BEYOND RELIGIONS

PETER KLEIN

BEYOND RELIGIONS

WHERE ARE WE HEADING
IN THE 21ST CENTURY?

ISBN : Paperback – 978-0-6482581-3-1
       E-Book – 978-0-6482581-2-4

Typeset by Reality Premedia Pvt. Ltd.

ALSO BY PETER KLEIN

Beyond God: Why Religions Are False,
Outdated and Dangerous

CONTENTS

PREFACE

When I wrote my first book, *Beyond God: Why Religions Are False, Outdated and Dangerous*, the word "dangerous" was included in the subtitle for a number of reasons – in particular because the book highlighted the many evils perpetrated over the centuries in the name of religions, including wars waged against adherents of other religions, subjugation of women, tolerance of slavery, and abhorrent treatment of homosexuals.

As I sit here writing this book during the Covid-19, or coronavirus, pandemic, a new danger caused by the religious mindset has become apparent. Religious groups around the world are being disproportionately affected by the virus because they regularly disobey advice from healthcare experts, including the World Health Organization (WHO), to self-isolate and avoid large gatherings. Church leaders (especially in America), imams in many Muslim nations, and Jewish prayer groups across the world have continued to encourage their followers to attend services; not only is this leading to sickness and death among adult members of their communities, but it is also infecting innocent children, as well as people their followers subsequently come into contact with.

The virus's heavy toll among these groups is a direct result of their leaders' disregard for state and international health authorities, bans on accessing mass media and, crucially, their rejection of science and scientific methods. Many members of strict religious orders have been isolated from information about the real world for much of their lives, and so will not accept advice from outside their communal teachings. "God will look after me," they say. Some refuse to wear masks because they "interfere with God's beautifully designed breathing system"; others believe the virus is retribution from God for "evil" behaviour.

As a result of this ignorance, children have had to bury their parents and families have been decimated. And yet the truth is it is a manageable infectious agent that is causing this modern-day plague. It behoves us to not waste life needlessly and recklessly, even if our knowledge and treatment of the virus is still developing. It is a sad indictment of society and religions that people can hold such fervent opinions, despite all evidence pointing to them being false and unfounded.

Many friends and acquaintances I chat with who identify with a religious group point out that their religion has been around for thousands of years and will continue to endure. While I admire their confidence, history is not on their side. The Sumerians, the Ancient Egyptians, the Greek and Roman empires and many other long-lasting dynasties believed that their existence and their gods would be eternal, but all that now remains of them are ruined buildings, some original texts, and historical accounts of their rise and fall.

The strictest religious sects are the last strongholds of traditional religions. More casual, less observant followers are rapidly becoming more secular as they are exposed to a much broader base of knowledge. This is particularly the case among young people. The World Wide Web has rapidly and dramatically increased access to information. The internet will eventually penetrate even the most cloistered communities and their young will no longer be kept in the dark by religious leaders determined to close them off from the world outside.

In the past, nations and religions were relatively isolated and segregated, with low rates of intermingling and intermarriage. But since the end of World War II and the growth of air travel, the world has become a melting-pot of cultures and religions. With this often comes the realization that one's own religion and culture are not necessarily "true" and others "false" – a teaching common to most religions. Being exposed to other cultures is leading people to question their religious leaders.

It is the intent of this book to project recent trends in religious adherence forwards a few decades to attempt to predict and understand what humanity's near future might look like. It will also reflect on how we can continue to develop and improve aspects of our lives that were once the sole preserve of religions, such as societal beliefs, communal living, ethical values and spiritual nourishment. We as a species need to determine how to replace positive aspects of religion and find ways to fulfil many of the same needs that gave rise to religions in the first place – needs that must still be met to ensure human happiness and well-being.

In order for us to project forwards, however, it is essential to have an initial understanding of how we have reached where we are today with regards belief systems.

CHAPTER 1

WHY ARE WE HERE?

From an amoeba to a plant to an antelope, all living things have inbuilt mechanisms that help them survive in their particular environment, reproduce, and pass on their genetic information to the next generation. As the most adept species on this planet, *Homo sapiens* further developed the capacity to ponder, predict, communicate and prepare for eventualities.

Wherever groups of humans settled, they almost always developed belief systems involving rituals and practices directed towards sacred objects or beings. These systems provided a way to explain and cope with things that seemed to be inexplicable, such as the cycles of the Sun and Moon, or events that were often terrifying or devastating, such as storms, earthquakes, floods, droughts, volcanic eruptions, sicknesses and, of course, death.

Whether these were religions depends on how you define a religion – for many people today a religion must be focused on a deity, and we do not always know if ancient belief systems involved the worship of a god or gods. But they clearly paved the way for modern-day religions.

One of the distinguishing features of *Homo sapiens* is our primal drive to make sense of what is going on around us. For the last 100,000-plus years, we have preferred an incorrect answer to no answer, as a way to provide comfort and structure to our lives. As a result of this, we have, at various times, worshipped aspects and concepts:
- of the earth (volcanoes, weather events, earthquakes)

- on the earth (animals, mountains and so on) and now
- above the earth

As early humans began to realize that neither things of the earth nor on the earth were likely to be controlling authorities, they subsequently invented gods – intangible forces that could more easily be attributed with supernatural powers.

A common thought among many primal cultures must have been "Who was the first mother or father?" To answer this question, many cultures invented one or more original creator beings. Unsurprisingly, over time these beings began to take on more anthropomorphic characteristics. The current monotheistic religions portray their being as an "invisible man in the sky" and call him "God" or a similar name.

As humans progressed through the Scientific Age, increasing numbers of people began questioning the validity of the idea of an all-knowing creator, and the more inquiring among them sought testable real-world answers to the questions they were asking, which gradually began to supplant the "deity hypotheses".

One of the questions that humans commonly ask is an existential one: why are we here? The major religions require that this issue be front and centre of any discussions about the meaning of life, as it helps them maintain their influence over society. They have begun admitting that science can explain the "how" of existence but assert that it can't provide the "why" – and that this is where religions believe they play a vital role. Religions cling to this purpose but assign it an importance well out of proportion to what it truly provides. Atheists, on the other hand, do not require a deity to be introduced into the equation. They look for and find meaning in everyday aspects of life. They can flippantly respond, "Why does your god need to exist?" and move on.

What happens to religions over time?

During the Paleolithic Age, ritualistic burials and customs were manifestations of the earliest belief systems. These were often superseded by animistic and shamanistic belief systems, which may have lasted for tens of thousands of years before being gradually replaced by deistic and theistic belief systems.

Hundreds of religions have developed and thrived before becoming extinct, often as a result of natural calamities, wars, invasions, mass conversions, or being subsumed by newer religions or rejected as a result of people gaining a clearer understanding of the natural world. Of the many hundreds and possibly even thousands of organized belief systems that have existed around the world, currently there are eleven with more than 4 million adherents: Christianity, Islam, Hinduism, Buddhism, Chinese folk religion, Sikhism, Spiritism, Judaism, Bahai, Jainism and Shinto.

Some of those that have, for all intents and purposes, disappeared are the

1. Ancient Chinese religions
2. Minoan religion
3. Greco-Roman religion
4. Ancient Egyptian religion
5. Babylonian religion
6. Norse religion
7. Celtic religion
8. Incan religion
9. Aztec religion
10. Mayan religion
11. Germanic, Slavic and Baltic polytheisms
12. Pacific island religions

What makes current religious rituals different from the ancient ones that we look back at with irreverence? Surprisingly little, if we examine such practices carefully – even though the associated religions have wider penetration, more developed and complex structures and large physical and financial presences.

Yet at the same time, none of the older religions that endure today are practised as they were in the early days of their existence and, indeed, they have often changed considerably in the last few hundred years. Though their main foundational texts are still perpetuated, the interpretation of them has altered and the way that festivities are celebrated has often changed quite extensively. After all, Jesus certainly knew nothing of Santa Claus, Christmas trees and carols.

When we consider all of this, it becomes apparent that we have created so many gods and religions throughout our history because we are more at ease and find more comfort in false answers than we do in having no answers. Moving forwards, will modern-day humanity become more willing to accept no answer rather than false ones? One would hope that we are reaching that point. After all, having no answer provides us with the freedom to properly test all hypotheses and consider all the evidence, which might eventually result in true understanding. Having no answer may be discomforting to a religious mind, but can be exciting for a secular mind!

So, where are we heading? When one looks objectively at the changes in religions over time, the words of the late Christopher Hitchens ring true: "From a plurality of Prime Movers the monotheists have bargained it down to a single one. They are getting ever nearer to the true round figure."[1]

CHAPTER 2

Science versus religion: Evidence versus Faith

We are only in the very early stages of the Scientific Age, yet we have achieved many more and greater advances in this last one hundred years than in the prior thousands of years under the direction of religious teachings – whether it be in the form of higher standards of living, technological innovations or the spread of equality and human rights. As described in my previous book, humankind has passed through the so-called magical phase, during which there were no rational explanations for phenomena, and the religious phase, during which the concept of an overseeing deity was the overriding explanation for most phenomena, to finally reach the scientific phase of our development.

We are currently in the middle of the first major pandemic in over a century. Prior to the Scientific Age, religions held sway over public opinion as to the causes and treatments of disease. Thankfully today the overwhelming majority of the global population have begun to embrace the scientific method and are now relying on epidemiologists, medical care and researchers to find a vaccine as the best way to deal with our current crisis. World leaders no longer rely on advice and guidance from religious leaders and instead, a reasonable amount of government Covid-19 press conference time has been allocated to scientific experts. The power of evidence-based systems is rapidly diminishing the relevance of religions as a source of information.

It is of interest to consider how religions have dealt with similar situations in the past. The Black Death plague of the mid-1300s was the deadliest pandemic in recorded history. It led to the deaths of between 75 million and 200 million people in Asia, the Middle East, North Africa and Europe – up to one quarter of the world's population. Leaders of all affected religions would often identify the sinfulness of humanity as the source of the plague. They preached that wickedness was being punished by their by god because people had not obeyed his orders – in other words, the cause was moral rather than microbial – and they never had difficulty locating verses in their sacred texts that provided 'evidence' for this.

When science was in its infancy, if it dared to show that religious teachings were wrong, religious authorities would not hesitate to wield their power to exterminate opposition. Giordano Bruno is one of the most famous early martyrs to the cause of science against religion. In 1600 he was burned alive at the stake after being found guilty of heresy by the Catholic Church. In 1633, another scientist, Galileo Galilei was pronounced to be "vehemently suspect of heresy" and condemned to house arrest for the rest of his life.

Despite the rise of science from the 18th century onwards and the proliferation of rational explanations for natural phenomena, religious institutions continued to resist the elevation of science to the same level of prestige as religion. For most religious leaders, scientists, like all humans, are flawed and cannot rival their deity, and so the aggrandizement of scientists was akin to creating to false gods.

Even today, these views endure and "science makes mistakes" is a common catch-cry among religious leaders. The former President of the United States, Donald Trump, often relied on his "gut feeling" instead of accepting advice and scientific evidence from professionals and researchers. In an attempt to garner support from religious groups, on 1 June 2020, in the middle of the pandemic, he posed with a Bible in front of St John's Episcopal Church in Washington as people nearby protested against his policies and thousands of his citizens continued to die. This and other pro-religious gestures by Trump have emboldened zealots, encouraged citizens to ignore scientific recommendations, and contributed to devastating outcomes across the United States.

Sadly, the advent of evidence-based medicine has done little to affect the way that religions deal with disease. Though often embracing modern care, many religious leaders, especially in developing nations, continue to favour and encourage the use of their most controlling but ineffective system: prayer. A tremendous number of children die each year, including in the United States, because parents keep sick children at home and pray for them instead of taking them to the local hospital just down the road. When all you have is a hammer, everything looks like a nail.

Scepticism towards science fomented by religious leaders has allowed dangerous unscientific attitudes and treatments to prevail in some communities. For example, most US states allow for religious exemptions from vaccinations. In 1945, the leaders of the Jehovah's Witnesses decided to impose a ban on blood transfusions – whole blood or any of its four major components (red cells, white cells, platelets and plasma). This doctrine is based on a few biblical quotes, including the following from Leviticus 17:10-12:

> I will set my face against any Israelite or any foreigner residing among them who eats blood, and I will cut them off from the people. For the life of a creature is in the blood, and I have given it to you to make atonement for yourselves on the altar; it is the blood that makes atonement for one's life. Therefore I say to the Israelites, "None of you may eat blood, nor may any foreigner residing among you eat blood."

Many people, including innocent children raised within the religion (of which there are currently 8 million adherents), have suffered or died needlessly as a result of this proscription.

Conversion therapy is a practice that has been adopted by some religious groups to "treat" people who are homosexual or transgender. It is based on the notion that these people are suffering from a disease of the mind, are committing a crime and sin against their god, and can be saved if forced to abandon their inclinations. Alan Turing, the famous mathematician, computer scientist and cryptanalyst was forced to undergo chemical castration – a year-long process of hormone injections. Other conversion treatments have included aversive therapies such as the application of electric shocks, the administration of nausea-inducing drugs while the subject is made to look at same-sex erotic images, psychoanalysis, and so on. Such treatments are rejected as dangerous and ineffective by every mainstream medical and mental health organization, yet many religious communities put pressure on adherents, who are often just teenagers, to go through this harmful process, and in many places across the globe conversion therapy is still a legal form of treatment.

As a result of religious teachings, millions of people around the world have died unnecessarily since the 1980s from HIV/AIDS. Zealots preach that the disease is a retribution from their god for the "sinful behaviour" of the gay community and discourage the use of condoms, the use of which saves countless lives.

Will history keep repeating itself if we allow religions to interfere with essential preventive healthcare advice? How many more people must suffer and die unnecessarily if religions maintain any power?

If most of us still relied on religious teachings as a source of information, we would be suffering terribly during the current pandemic and every other outbreak of disease. Fortunately, science continues to highlight the lack of evidence for most religious teachings; at the same time scholars repeatedly show that the foundational stories on which most religions are based are in fact fabrications, misapprehensions or allegories.

While the scientific process continues to demonstrate an ever-greater understanding of the natural world, religious teachings of "miracles" and "the power of prayer" are having to be reshaped and thankfully are on a pathway towards elimination. As will be seen in the following chapter, trust in science over religion is steadily increasing. What's more, rarely do people revert to religion in their attempts to understand, thrive and survive in the world. So the falsehoods and divisive teachings of religions are being left behind. To paraphrase Neil DeGrasse-Tyson, it is now evident that "god is an ever-receding pocket of scientific ignorance"[2] and it is essential that we distance ourselves from such dangerous views.

CHAPTER 3

CURRENT TRAJECTORIES

Over the centuries, humankind has steadily reduced thousands of local belief systems down to a handful of predominant organized religions in the early 21st century. How are religions likely to develop from here, and where do modern humans now seek facts and guidance on how to live?

Fortunately, we not only have snapshot data available to assess where we are right now but also some studies that have been running for decades. Let's begin by looking at the data from the countries that have created the most wide-ranging surveys. These are the more economically advanced and liberated societies, where the relevant questions can be asked quite freely.

The United States

Looking at a number of recent surveys in the United States, religiosity is decreasing, though with a slight lag compared to many other Western countries. In October 2019, the Pew Research Centre released its latest update on America's changing religious landscape, entitled "In U.S., Decline of Christianity Continues at Rapid Pace". It also released its latest "Religious Landscape Study" in 2015, based on data from more than 35,000 Americans from all 50 states.

A brief summary of some of the data from both studies is as follows:
1. Belief in "God" dropped from 71% to 63% in the seven years between the 2007 and 2014 studies (Image 1).

2. In 2019, 65% of Americans described themselves as Christian, down from 77% ten years earlier (Image 2).
3. The percentage of people declaring themselves to be religiously unaffiliated (atheist/agnostic/nothing in particular) has risen from 17% to 26% in those same ten years (Image 2).
4. Frequency of attendance at church among those who still identify as belonging to a religion has declined from 54% in 2007 to 45% in 2019 (Image 3).
5. Frequency of attendance at church rapidly declines by age group: 60% of those in the Silent Generation (born 1928–45) attend more than once a month, but only 35% of Millennials (born 1981–96) attend at this frequency (Image 4).
6. The older population is far more likely to be religiously affiliated than the younger generations. In fact, when looking at the "unaffiliated" group, only 10% of those in the Silent Generation are unaffiliated whereas 40% of Millennials are not connected with religion – a remarkable four-fold increase (Image 4). In number terms, taking into account the increase in population size, the religiously unaffiliated category has increased from 39 million in 2009 to 68 million in 2019.
7. Belief in a god decreases markedly with age. In those aged 65 and over, 70% believe, but for those aged 18–29 this drops to 51% (Image 5).

Belief in God
% of adults who say they...

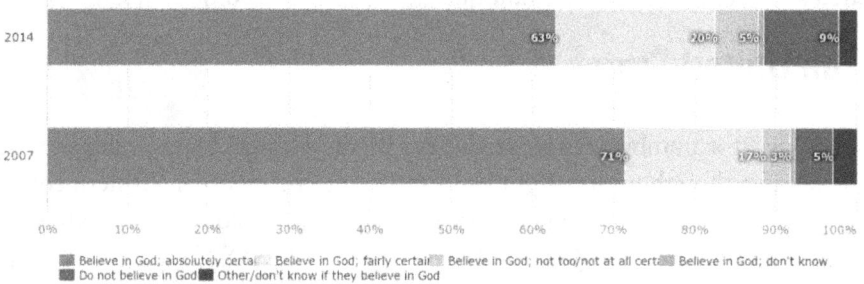

Image 1

In U.S., smaller share of adults identify as Christians, while religious 'nones' have grown

% of U.S. adults who identify as ...

... Christian

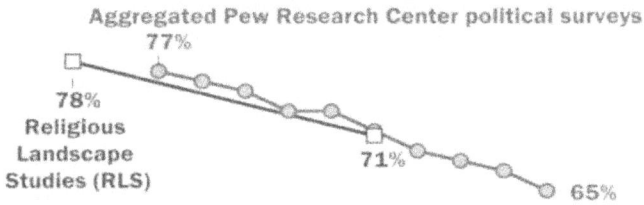

... religiously unaffiliated

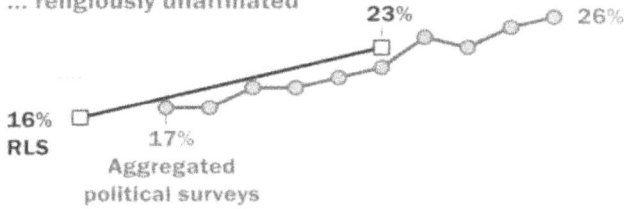

Source: Pew Research Center Religious Landscape Studies (2007 and 2014). Aggregated Pew Research Center political surveys conducted 2009-July 2019 on the telephone.
"In U.S., Decline of Christianity Continues at Rapid Pace"

PEW RESEARCH CENTER

Image 2

In U.S., church attendance is declining

% of U.S. adults who say they attend religious services ...

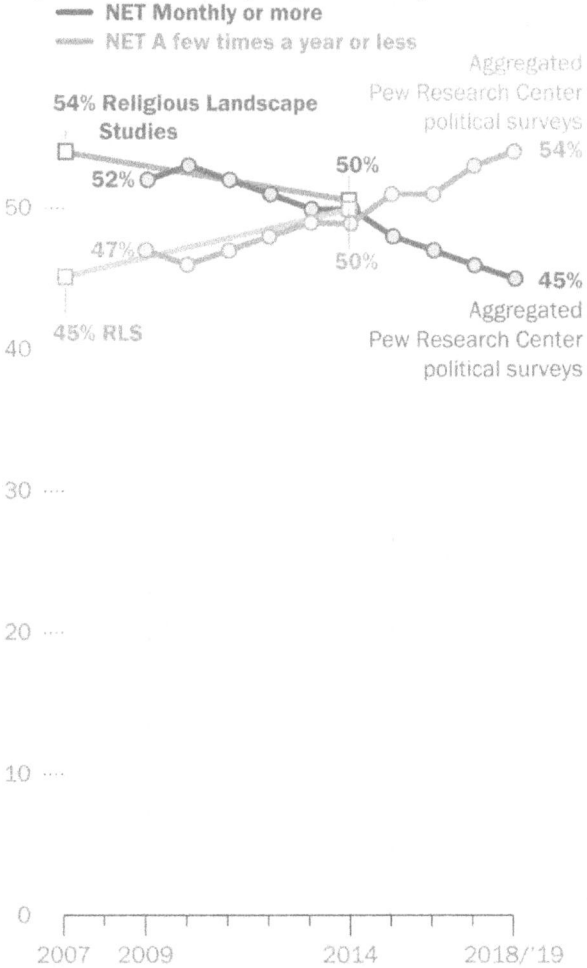

— NET Monthly or more

— NET A few times a year or less

54% Religious Landscape
Studies

Aggregated
Pew Research Center
political surveys

52%

50%

54%

47%

50%

45%

45% RLS

Aggregated
Pew Research Center
political surveys

50

40

30

20

10

0

2007 2009 2014 2018/'19

Source: Pew Research Center Religious Landscape Studies (2007
and 2014). Aggregated Pew Research Center political surveys
conducted 2009-July 2019 on the telephone.
"In U.S., Decline of Christianity Continues at Rapid Pace"

PEW RESEARCH CENTER

Image 3

The charts below suggest that once the Silent Generation and Baby Boomers are no longer with us, the majority of the population will have no religious affiliation and little interest in attending religious services.

Large generation gap in American religion

In 2018/2019, % of U.S. adults who identify as ...

	Christian	Non-Christian faiths	Unaffiliated
Silent Generation (born 1928-45)	84%	4%	10%
Baby Boomers (1946-64)	76	6	17
Generation X (1965-80)	67	6	25
Millennials (1981-96)	49	9	40

In 2018/2019, % of U.S. adults who say they attend religious services ...

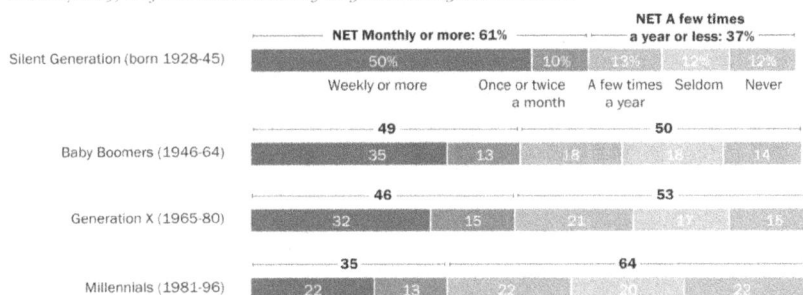

NET Monthly or more: 61% — NET A few times a year or less: 37%

	Weekly or more	Once or twice a month	A few times a year	Seldom	Never
Silent Generation (born 1928-45)	50%	10%	13%	12%	12%
Baby Boomers (1946-64) [49 / 50]	35	13	18	18	14
Generation X (1965-80) [46 / 53]	32	15	21	17	15
Millennials (1981-96) [35 / 64]	22	13	22	20	22

Note: Don't know/refused not shown.
Source: Aggregated Pew Research Center political surveys conducted January 2018-July 2019 on the telephone.
"In U.S., Decline of Christianity Continues at Rapid Pace"

PEW RESEARCH CENTER

Image 4

Belief in God by age group (2014)

% of adults who say they...

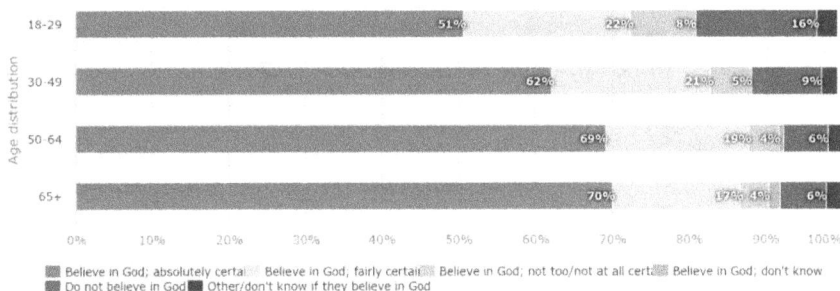

Age distribution				
18-29	51%	22%	8%	16%
30-49	62%	21%	5%	9%
50-64	69%	19%	4%	6%
65+	70%	17%	4%	6%

0% 10% 20% 30% 40% 50% 60% 70% 80% 90% 100%

Believe in God; absolutely certain Believe in God; fairly certain Believe in God; not too/not at all certain Believe in God; don't know
Do not believe in God Other/don't know if they believe in God

Image 5

The figures for Generation Z (born 1997–2012) are not shown on the above graph but are revealed in the following chart. They indicate an ever-increasing secularization among the young and even less interest in religion compared to all of those who preceded them, and show that 35% of this group are atheist, agnostic or not religious.

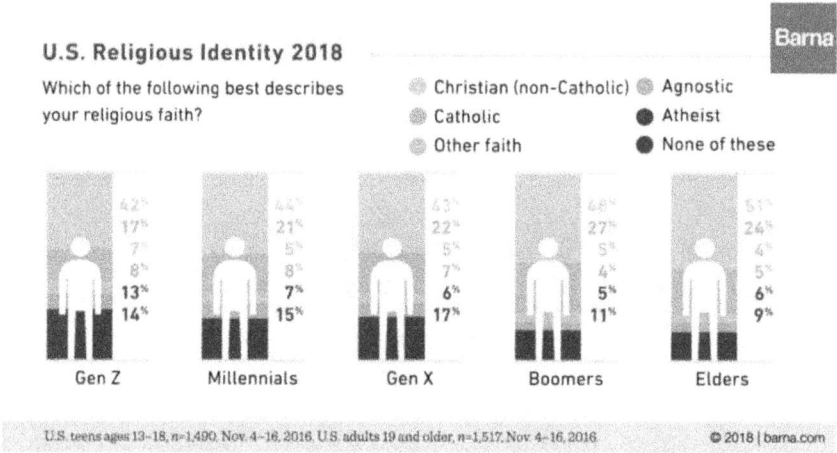

U.S. Religious Identity 2018   Barna

Which of the following best describes   ● Christian (non-Catholic) ● Agnostic
your religious faith?   ● Catholic   ● Atheist
                                               ● Other faith   ● None of these

42%	44%	43%	68%	51%
17%	21%	22%	27%	24%
7%	5%	5%	5%	4%
8%	8%	7%	4%	5%
13%	7%	6%	5%	6%
14%	15%	17%	11%	9%
Gen Z	Millennials	Gen X	Boomers	Elders

U.S. teens ages 13–18, n=1,490. Nov. 4–16, 2016. U.S. adults 19 and older, n=1,517. Nov. 4–16, 2016.   © 2018 | barna.com

Image 6

Importance of religion in one's life by generational group

% of adults who say religion is...

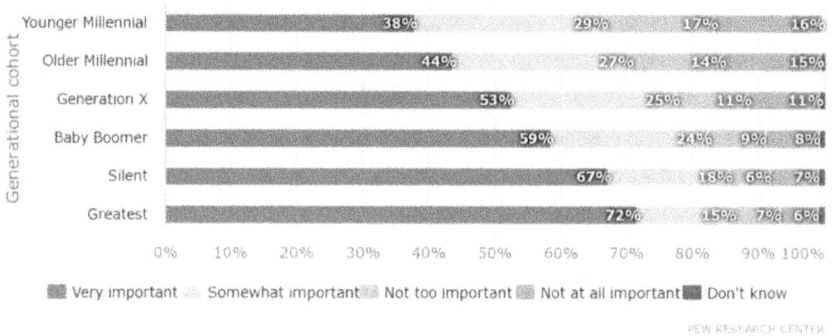

Generational cohort				
Younger Millennial	38%	29%	17%	16%
Older Millennial	44%	27%	14%	15%
Generation X	53%	25%	11%	11%
Baby Boomer	59%	24%	9%	8%
Silent	67%	18%	6%	7%
Greatest	72%	15%	7%	6%

0%   10%   20%   30%   40%   50%   60%   70%   80%   90% 100%

■ Very important ■ Somewhat important ■ Not too important ■ Not at all important ■ Don't know

PEW RESEARCH CENTER

Image 7

The United Kingdom

Despite the fact that its official religion is Christianity, its monarch is the head of the Anglican Church and its national anthem is "God Save the Queen", the United Kingdom is an increasingly secular society – indeed, one of the most secular nations on the planet.

The following statistics come from the 2018 edition of the "British Social Attitudes Survey", a detailed annual report from the National Centre for Social Research, based in London, which is now up to its 36th edition. It is a comprehensive analysis of the UK population, covering a variety of topics. A large section is devoted to assessing where belief systems fit within the society and how data has changed over recent decades.

In the section entitled "Religion – Identity, Behaviour and Belief over Two Decades", the opening remarks on this subject are:

> The past two decades have seen international conflict involving religion and domestic religious organisations putting themselves at odds with mainstream values. Against this backdrop, we compare religious identification, behaviour and belief among the British public. We find a dramatic decline in identification with Christian denominations, particularly the Church of England; a substantial increase in atheism and in self-description as "very" or "extremely" non-religious; and very low confidence in religious organisations, but tolerance of religious difference.[3]

The first graph in that section of the report assesses the changes in identification with religions from 1983 to 2018.

Religious identity, 1983–2018

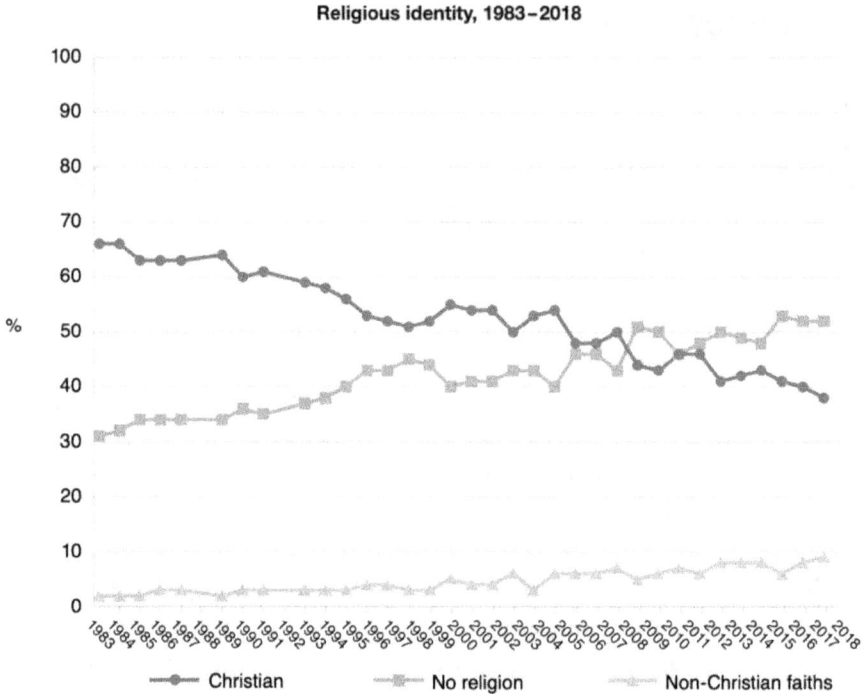

Image 8

As can be seen, in the United Kingdom there has been a significant decrease in the number of people associating themselves with Christianity and a massive increase in those who no longer identify with religion. In fact, the majority of Britons are now of "No religion".

As to changes with age, there is a similar trend to that seen globally, with young people being far less affiliated than their elders. The drop-off is happening to a much broader age range as well as to a much greater extent than in the United States, with the rapid decline commencing at those aged under 54.

Church of England/Anglican affiliation, by age

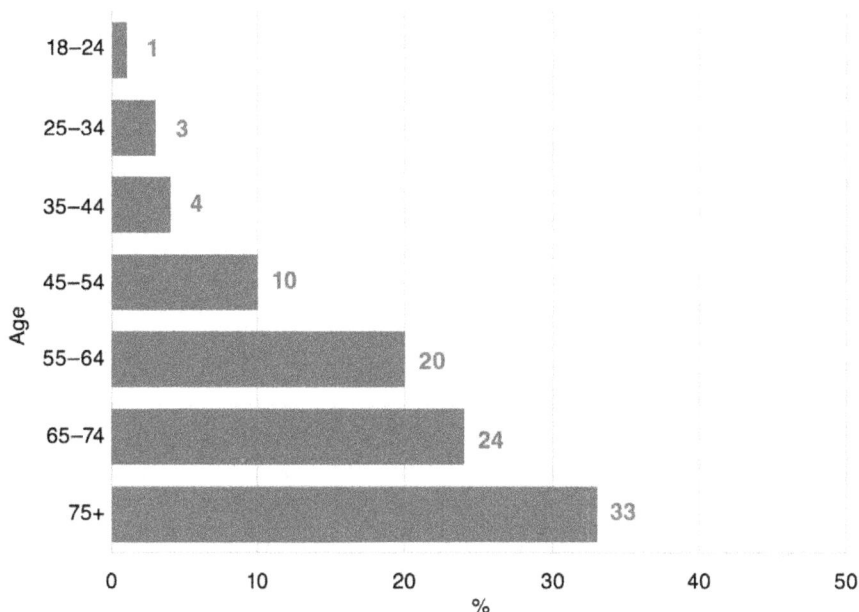

Image 9

Assessing the data further reveals that the number of people raised in a religious household who now self-report as having no religion has increased from 11% in 1998 to 23% in 2018 (the remainder of those who identify as non-religious had already been raised in non-religious households). It also shows that many people who were previously equivocal about religion have shifted to being "Very or extremely non-religious" (Image 10).

Table 2 Self-assessed religiosity, 1998-2018

	1998	2008	2018
Describing oneself as...	%	%	%
Very or extremely religious	6	7	7
Somewhat religious	31	30	24
Neither religious nor non-religious	30	23	19
Somewhat non-religious	13	11	11
Very or extremely non-religious	14	27	33
Unweighted base	*807*	*1986*	*1552*

Image 10

Praying has always been the mainstay of religious practice, but coinciding with the reduction in identification with religion, there has also been a decrease in the number of people who pray. Officially half of the United Kingdom now never prays. Although there has been an increase in those who pray several times a day, this is likely to be directly associated with the increase of the Muslim population.

Table 5 Frequency of prayer, 1998-2018

	1998	2008	2018
How often pray	%	%	%
Never	30	41	50
'Occasional' (less than once a week) ‡	41	34	29
Every week	5	3	3
Several times a week	6	5	4
Once a day	10	8	6
Several times a day	5	5	8
Unweighted base	*807*	*1986*	*1552*

‡ *'Occasional' (less than once a week) combines the answers: "Less often than once a year", "About once or twice a year", "Several times a year", "About once a month", "2-3 times a month", "Nearly every week"*

Image 11

Considering the UK data by age group, as we did for the figures from the United States, it's clear that today's younger generations are far more removed from religion than their elders. As the older generations pass away, the percentage of people who actively participate in religion will continue to recede.

Religious identification, attendance and belief in God by age, by gender

	Male	Female	All
% Have a religion			
18-34	32	41	36
35-54	37	50	43
55+	51	65	58
All ages	41	54	47
% Ever attends religious services or meetings*			
18-34	26	32	29
35-54	28	35	32
55+	29	37	33
All ages	28	35	31
% Believe in God‡			
18-34	29	38	33
35-54	36	44	40
55+	33	50	42
All ages	33	45	39

Image 12

Science and religion are often seen as being at opposing ends of the spectrum; the former deals with evidence and the latter usually relies on faith. While religions are being forced to accept some scientific findings, faith is never brought into the scientific process. A question in the survey has pointedly demonstrated a drastic shift in the acceptance of scientific thinking and the veracity of its methodology over that of faith.

In 1993, just under half agreed with the statement that "we believe too often in science and not enough in feelings and faith", but as of 2018 just

27% agree. It would be even more interesting if this question were untangled so as to separate "faith" and "feelings". Feelings will and should continue to be a part of who we are and help define our sentient nature. If the answer were simplified to "we believe too often in science and not enough in faith", I believe the graph would display even sharper trends.

Agreement that "we believe too often in science and not enough in feelings and faith", 1993–2018

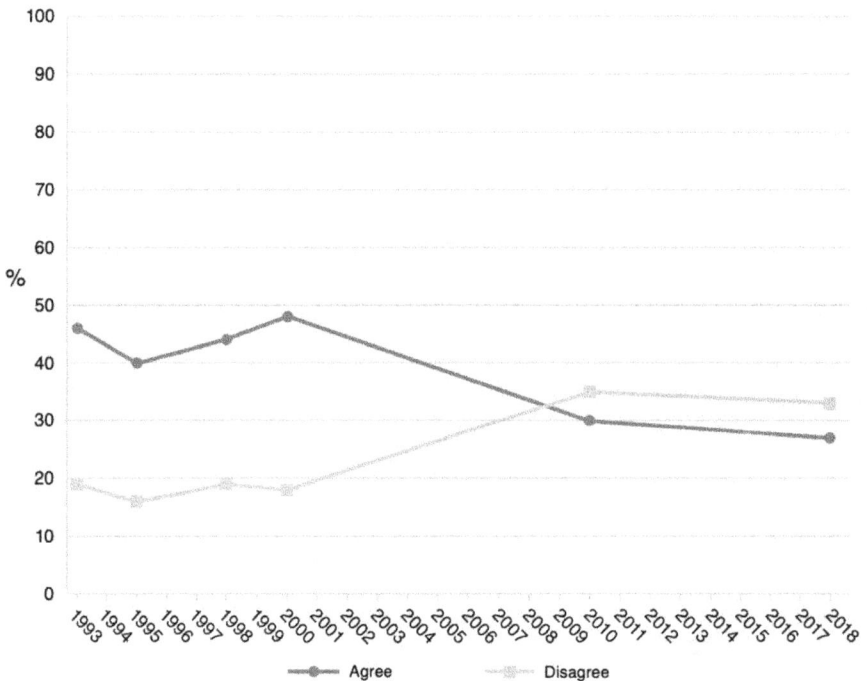

Image 13

Another part of the survey assessed how much confidence the population has in some of the most essential societal systems. Despite the protracted and painful Brexit fiasco, "Churches and religious organisations" rated even more poorly than "Parliament" with regards to "No confidence at all" (Image 14).

Confidence in Institutions

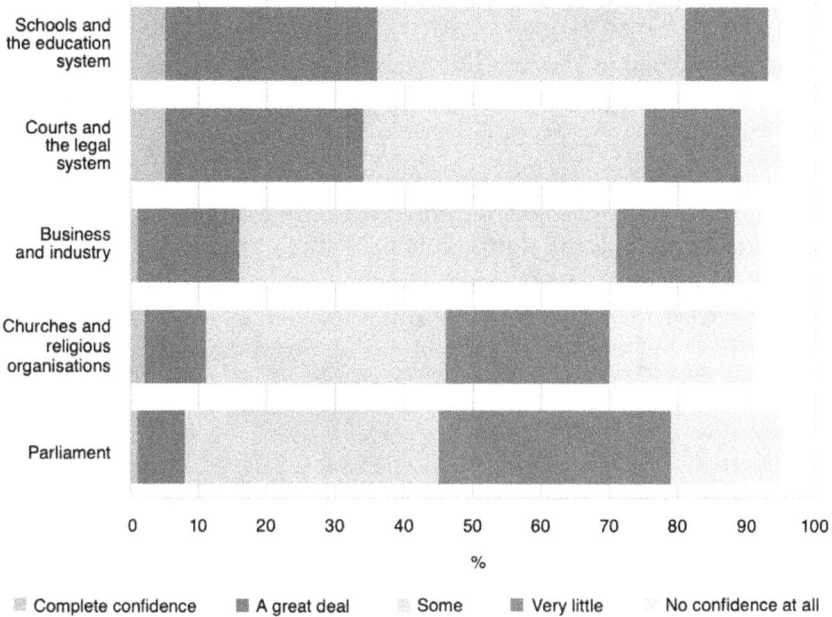

Image 14

All these indicators underline the variety of ways in which religion in the United Kingdom is suffering a rapid reduction in its relevance to the country's citizens.

Western Europe

Despite an increase in migration into Western Europe from parts of Asia and Africa, the overwhelming majority of the population is still Christian. Some countries are predominantly Catholic, such as Italy, Spain and Portugal, while others are predominantly Protestant, for example the United Kingdom and the Scandinavian countries.

An extensive Pew Research survey released in 2018, "Being Christian in Western Europe", showed increasing rates of non-belief among both umbrella groups of Christianity. The survey also indicated that among those who continue to identify as Christian there is a rapidly decreasing connection with the practice of Christianity. Fewer people who still consider themselves

Christian attend church, pray or believe literally in the god of the Bible. This suggests that when people answer a simple question about their religion, responding "Christian" is often more out of habit than belief.

Indeed, religion in Western Europe is increasingly becoming a historical and cultural artefact rather than a modern-day practice. This is evidenced by following images and tables from the Pew Research survey.

Share of 'nones' in Western Europe ranges from 15% in Ireland, Italy and Portugal to 48% in the Netherlands

% who say they are atheist, agnostic or have no particular religion

☐ 0-15% ■ 16-25% ■ 26-39% ■ 40%+   ☐ Non-surveyed country

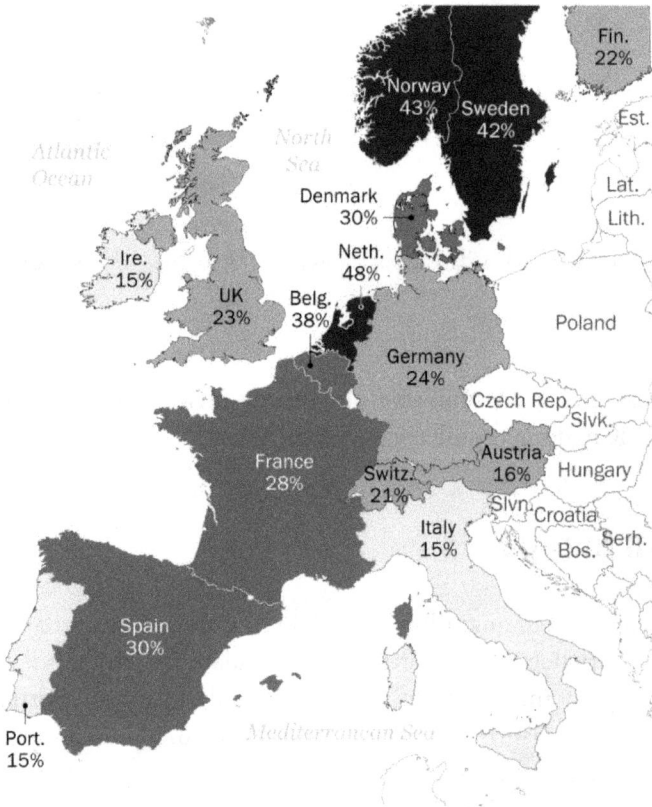

Note: Respondents were asked "What is your present religion, if any? Are you Christian, Muslim, Jewish, Buddhist, Hindu, atheist, agnostic, something else or nothing in particular?"
Source: Survey conducted April-August 2017 in 15 countries. See Methodology for details.
"Being Christian in Western Europe"

Image 15

In Western Europe, net losses for Christians are largely matched by gains for religiously unaffiliated

% who say they are/were ...

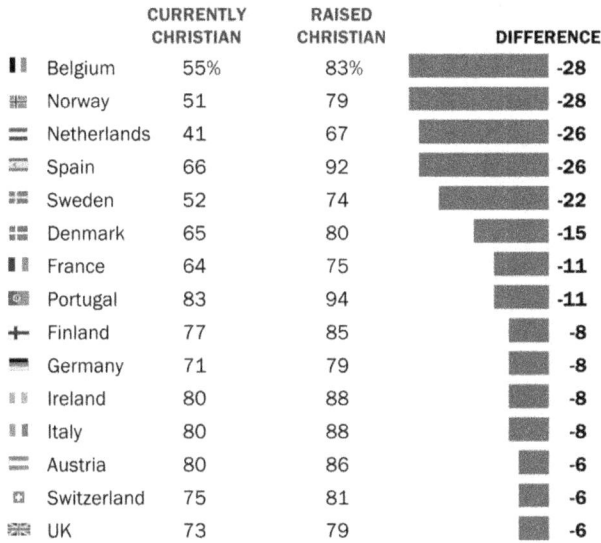

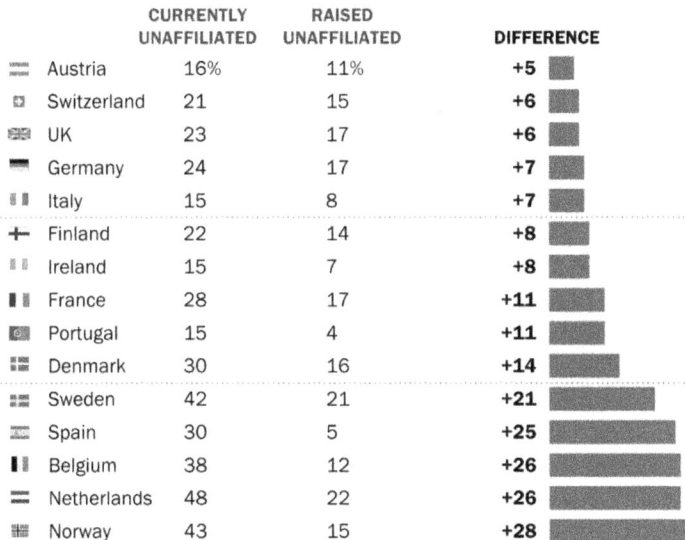

		CURRENTLY CHRISTIAN	RAISED CHRISTIAN	DIFFERENCE
▮▮	Belgium	55%	83%	-28
	Norway	51	79	-28
═	Netherlands	41	67	-26
▤	Spain	66	92	-26
	Sweden	52	74	-22
	Denmark	65	80	-15
▮▮	France	64	75	-11
	Portugal	83	94	-11
✛	Finland	77	85	-8
▬	Germany	71	79	-8
	Ireland	80	88	-8
▮▮	Italy	80	88	-8
═	Austria	80	86	-6
▣	Switzerland	75	81	-6
▨	UK	73	79	-6

		CURRENTLY UNAFFILIATED	RAISED UNAFFILIATED	DIFFERENCE
═	Austria	16%	11%	+5
▣	Switzerland	21	15	+6
▨	UK	23	17	+6
▬	Germany	24	17	+7
▮▮	Italy	15	8	+7
✛	Finland	22	14	+8
	Ireland	15	7	+8
▮▮	France	28	17	+11
	Portugal	15	4	+11
	Denmark	30	16	+14
	Sweden	42	21	+21
▤	Spain	30	5	+25
▮▮	Belgium	38	12	+26
═	Netherlands	48	22	+26
	Norway	43	15	+28

Note: Differences are calculated after rounding. All differences are statistically significant.
Source: Survey conducted April-August 2017 in 15 countries. See Methodology for details.
"Being Christian in Western Europe"

Image 16

Fewer than a quarter of people in most Western European countries show high levels of religious commitment

% who have _____ levels of religious commitment, according to a four-item index

	Low	Moderate	High
Portugal	30%	33%	37%
Italy	36	37	27
Ireland	41	34	24
Spain	55	24	21
Netherlands	64	19	18
Norway	61	22	17
Austria	49	38	14
Finland	62	26	13
France	58	29	12
Germany	53	36	12
Switzerland	52	37	12
United Kingdom	58	31	11
Belgium	68	22	10
Sweden	75	15	10
Denmark	69	23	8
MEDIAN	**58**	**29**	**13**

Note: The index is created by combining four individual measures of religious observance: self-assessment of religion's importance in one's life, religious attendance, prayer, and belief in God.

Image 17

A stark difference is seen here when comparing Catholic versus Protestant countries. The top four countries and the only ones where more than 20% of people have a high level of religious commitment are all predominantly Catholic nations (Image 17). It appears that the hold of the Catholic Church over its followers is stronger and more far-reaching than that of the Protestant Church. In these four nations, religious views still influence the secular legal code. For example, in Ireland "publication or utterance of blasphemous matter" was a criminal offence until January 2020, and in each of these countries Catholic teaching still has a strongly supported presence in public schools.

When assessing connectivity with a religion, one of the main factors to assess is attendance at religious services. In Western Europe, over half of the population "seldom or never" attend services. Even in Italy, Spain and Portugal, the most religious of the European countries, that's the case for around 40% of the population. (The corresponding figures in the United States are 24% for the Silent Generation, 32% for the Baby Boomers, 32% for Generation X and 42% for Millennials.[4])

Attending religious services 'seldom' or 'never' is the norm in Western Europe

% who say they attend religious services …

	Weekly/ monthly	A few times a year	Seldom/ never
Italy	43%	18%	39%
Ireland	37	22	41
Portugal	36	22	42
Austria	30	22	48
Switzerland	29	18	53
Germany	24	23	53
Spain	23	11	66
France	22	16	62
United Kingdom	20	22	58
Netherlands	18	18	64
Norway	16	24	60
Denmark	12	36	51
Belgium	11	20	68
Sweden	11	25	63
Finland	10	33	58
MEDIAN	**22**	**22**	**58**

Note: Don't know/refused responses not shown.
Source: Survey conducted April-August 2017 in 15 countries. See Methodology for details.
"Being Christian in Western Europe"

Image 18

Fully seven-in-ten in Denmark, Sweden say religion is not important to them

% who say religion is ____ important in their lives

	Very/ somewhat	Not too/not at all
Denmark	27%	72%
Sweden	27	72
Belgium	36	64
Finland	38	62
United Kingdom	40	60
France	42	57
Netherlands	44	56
Norway	46	54
Switzerland	47	53
Germany	47	52
Spain	49	50
Austria	51	49
Ireland	56	44
Italy	58	42
Portugal	72	27
MEDIAN	**46**	**54**

Note: Don't know/refused responses not shown.
Source: Survey conducted April-August 2017 in 15 countries. See Methodology for details. "Being Christian in Western Europe"

Image 19

It is eminently clear that religions are no longer relevant for an increasing proportion of the Western European population. Interestingly, one of the interests that is replacing religion is community involvement in sports: there is a shift from communal attendance at places of worship to communal attendance at sporting events. Thankfully this is good for the health of the body as well as the mind, and it connects people to tribalisms that are potentially less divisive or devastating than religions.

Highly committed Christians more likely than 'nones' to volunteer with community groups, but more 'nones' engaged in sports clubs

% of _____ who say, in the past month, they spent an hour or more of their time participating in ...

	Community group or neighborhood association				Sports or recreation club			
	Religiously unaffiliated	Christians with low levels of commitment	Christians with moderate levels of commitment	Highly committed Christians	Religiously unaffiliated	Christians with low levels of commitment	Christians with moderate levels of commitment	Highly committed Christians
Austria	10%	13%	15%	30%	43%	38%	34%	35%
Belgium	21	23	24	37	45	48	51	30
Denmark	21	22	34	34	41	46	37	42
Finland	25	24	27	37	32	34	36	31
France	17	13	16	18	39	38	31	31
Germany	9	14	17	22	39	43	33	34
Ireland	23	17	21	32	46	31	33	33
Italy	12	10	15	14	31	26	23	19
Netherlands	20	22	29	27	57	59	60	48
Norway	21	26	27	33	42	35	43	26
Portugal	13	9	8	13	31	26	22	19
Spain	18	13	19	28	34	32	25	27
Sweden	23	23	26	33	35	39	38	31
Switzerland	11	20	15	24	42	29	30	23
UK	12	11	11	19	39	26	30	22
MEDIAN	**18**	**17**	**19**	**28**	**39**	**35**	**33**	**31**

Note: Religious commitment is measured as an index of the following individual practices: attendance at religious services, importance of religion in one's life, frequency of prayer and belief in God. See Appendix A: Scaling and regression analysis for more details.
Source: Survey conducted April-August 2017 in 15 countries. See Methodology for details.
"Being Christian in Western Europe"

Image 20

One hypothesis to consider here is that other communal attachments increases when connectivity with religion decreases. The Pew Research study goes further and also demonstrates an increase in pride in one's national history and values as religious connection decreases. It may be that there is a limit to the number of substantive communal connections we can readily maintain.

Among Christians, pride in nationality more common than pride in religion

% of Christians who say they are very proud to be a national of their country (e.g. "to be Finnish")/ very proud to be a Christian

	Very proud to be a national of their country	Very proud to be Christian	Difference
Finland	63%	39%	+24
Austria	47	24	+23
Denmark	53	30	+23
Sweden	59	36	+23
Norway	67	45	+22
Ireland	56	36	+20
Switzerland	47	28	+19
United Kingdom	42	25	+17
France	46	31	+15
Germany	37	23	+14
Italy	50	36	+14
Belgium	40	27	+13
Netherlands	44	33	+11
Spain	60	50	+10
Portugal	72	67	+5
MEDIAN	**50**	**33**	

Note: All differences are statistically significant.
Source: Survey conducted April-August 2017 in 15 countries. See Methodology for details.
"Being Christian in Western Europe"

Image 21

Adherence to religious strictures can result in a narrow perspective and this is evident in the following data relating to acceptance of same-sex marriage. In the countries where there was public debate on the issue and potential changes to marriage laws were proposed, the strongest opposition came from religious adherents and their authorities. Churches and religious organizations across the globe committed substantial funds to the fight against same-sex marriage laws.

Highly observant Christians are less likely to favor same-sex marriage

% who strongly favor/favor allowing gays and lesbians to marry legally

	Religiously unaffiliated	Christians with low levels of commitment	Christians with moderate levels of commitment	Highly committed Christians
Austria	87%	87%	69%	34%
Belgium	88	85	81	57
Denmark	92	90	82	69
Finland	84	68	52	39
France	85	80	77	32
Germany	86	84	72	44
Ireland	87	86	67	35
Italy	83	78	60	35
Netherlands	95	91	90	60
Norway	83	80	68	39
Portugal	82	71	59	44
Spain	90	83	74	58
Sweden	94	90	91	64
Switzerland	89	80	75	41
UK	82	85	81	41
MEDIAN	**87**	**84**	**74**	**41**

Image 22

As discussed in more detail in my previous book, having a strong connection to one's religion often results in a more divisive and judgmental mindset. History has shown this to be true over and over again, in almost every nation and religion. In fact, not only can strict religious adherence affect one's perception of the practices of other religions, it can alter one's perception of other people's compatibility with the predominant culture of one's own country. For example, the graph below shows that, in nearly every country studied, Christians who attend church regularly are more likely to consider Islam incompatible with their nation's values.

Christians more likely than 'nones' to say Islam is incompatible with national values

% who say, "Islam is fundamentally incompatible with our country's culture and values"

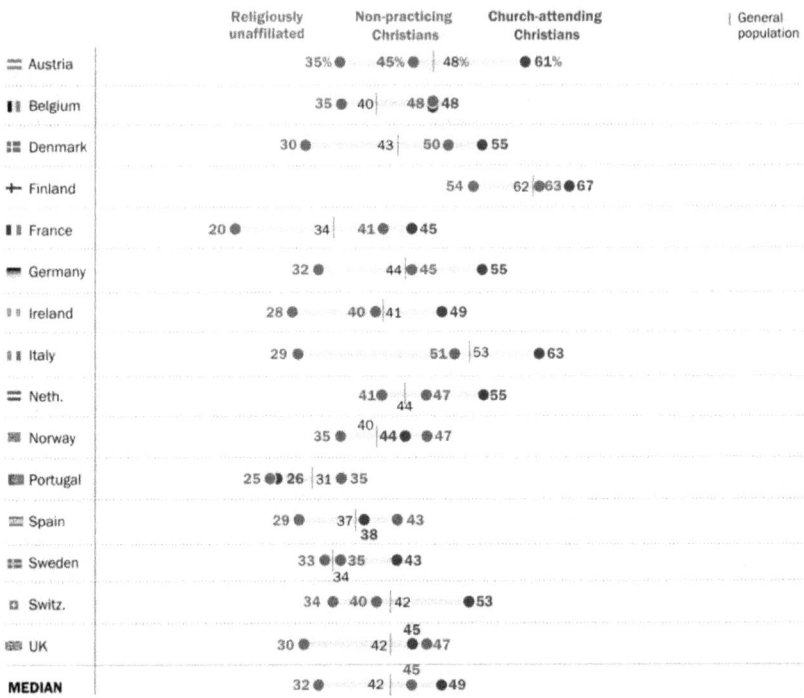

	Religiously unaffiliated	Non-practicing Christians	Church-attending Christians	General population
Austria	35% ●	45% ●	48% ● 61%	
Belgium	35 ●	40	48 ● 48	
Denmark	30 ●	43	50 ● ● 55	
Finland			54 ● 62 ● 63 ● 67	
France	20 ●	34	41 ● ● 45	
Germany	32 ●	44 ● 45	● 55	
Ireland	28 ●	40 ● 41	● 49	
Italy	29 ●	51 ● 53	● 63	
Neth.		41 ● 44 ● 47	● 55	
Norway	35 ●	40 44 ● ● 47		
Portugal	25 ● ● 26 31 ● 35			
Spain	29 ●	37 ● 38 ● 43		
Sweden	33 ● ● 35 34 ● 43			
Switz.	34 ●	40 ● 42 45	● 53	
UK	30 ●	42 ● ● 47 45		
MEDIAN	32 ●	42 ● ● 49		

Image 23

Consistent with trends seen in other nations, the study shows that those who are religiously unaffiliated turn to scientific and naturalistic explanations rather than religious or mystical teachings to understand the world. Throughout Western Europe, a half to two-thirds of religiously unaffiliated people surveyed say, "Science makes religion unnecessary in my life."

Most religiously unaffiliated Europeans say science makes religion unnecessary

% who completely/mostly agree with the statement, "Science makes religion unnecessary in my life"

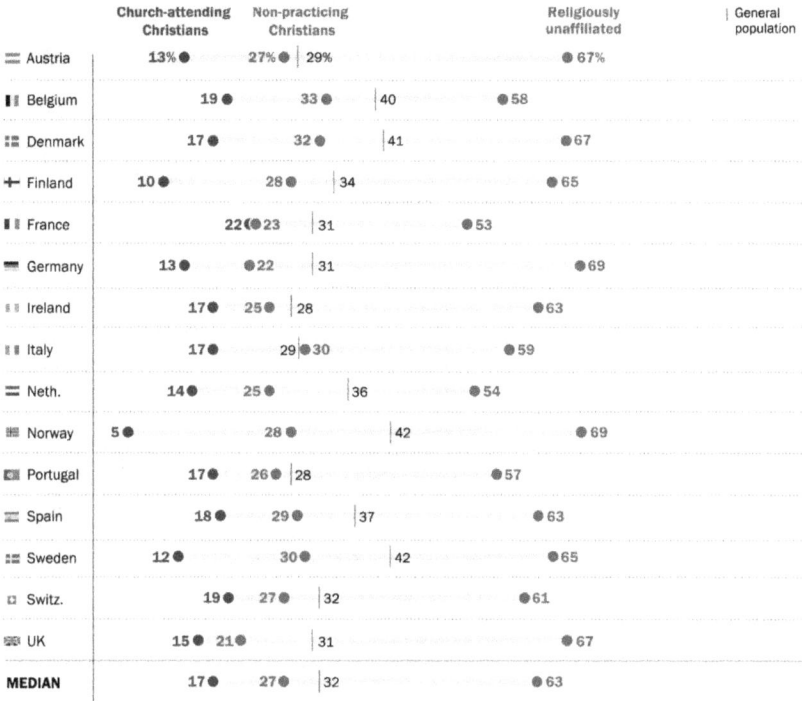

	Church-attending Christians	Non-practicing Christians	Religiously unaffiliated	General population
Austria	13%	27%	29%	67%
Belgium	19	33	40	58
Denmark	17	32	41	67
Finland	10	28	34	65
France	22	23	31	53
Germany	13	22	31	69
Ireland	17	25	28	63
Italy	17	29	30	59
Neth.	14	25	36	54
Norway	5	28	42	69
Portugal	17	26	28	57
Spain	18	29	37	63
Sweden	12	30	42	65
Switz.	19	27	32	61
UK	15	21	31	67
MEDIAN	17	27	32	63

Image 24

China

China has the world's largest population, at 1.4 billion people, and of that number approximately 92% belong to the Han Chinese ethnic group. Most of these people do not adhere to a deity-based dogmatic religion, though they often participate in folk religion practices. If one defines Buddhism and Confucianism as philosophies, especially when no deity is part of the practice, then China is the most atheistic country on the planet.

Percentage of the Chinese population with "No Religion"

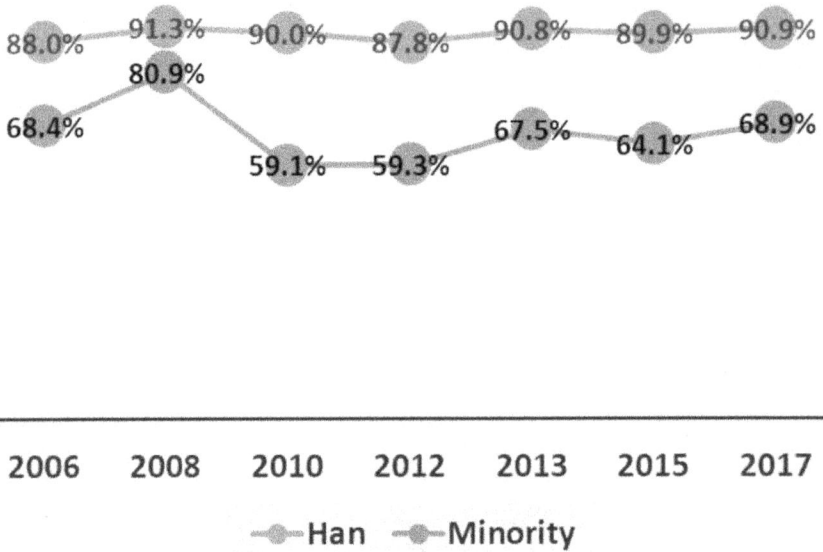

88.0% — 91.3% — 90.0% — 87.8% — 90.8% — 89.9% — 90.9%

80.9%

68.4%

67.5% — 64.1% — 68.9%

59.1% — 59.3%

| 2006 | 2008 | 2010 | 2012 | 2013 | 2015 | 2017 |

Han — Minority

Image 25

Religious belief in China

Religious Affiliations	Frequency	Percent
Buddhism	565	5.07
Islam	237	2.13
Christianity	191	1.71
Catholicism	38	0.34
Daoism	37	0.33
Folk Religions	211	1.89
Others	17	0.15
Non-believers	**9902**	**88.89**

Image 26

Alongside this data, one can see similar values in the more detailed analysis from the 2012 Win-Gallup worldwide poll (Image 33). Its results show that 30% of Chinese people polled define themselves as "non-religious", 47% are "convinced atheists" and only 14% declare themselves "a religious person" (9% responded "don't know" or gave no response). In a population of 1.4 billion people, this equates to over one billion people who are either non-religious or convinced atheists in China alone.

Japan

Religious adherents often claim that without a deity we have nowhere to obtain an objective moral code. Yet Japan, where more than two-thirds of citizens have no religion, is one of the most respectful cultures I have ever experienced. Children of a very young age freely walk the streets to and from school with minimal concern, while theft, crime and homicide figures are extremely low. With 125 million inhabitants, Japan is the eleventh most populous nation, yet according to the United Nations Office on Drugs and Crime, in 2018 its rate of intentional homicide per 100,000 was the second lowest in the world at 0.3 (Australia's was 0.9, Sweden's 1.1, the United Kingdom's 1.2 and America's 5).

A Pew Research survey in October 2017 found almost 70% of Japanese people report that they have no religious belief.[5] Although many people participate in Shinto rituals, they do not see themselves as members of an organized doctrinal religion. Shinto is not a monotheistic deity system but predominantly a pantheistic connection to the natural world.

In a different Pew Research survey ("The Age Gap in Religion around the World, 2008–2017"[6]), the percentage of people in Japan who stated that "religion is very important in their lives" was 10%. This figure is comparable to those recorded in the United Kingdom, Sweden and France; in the United States the result was 53%.

In the Japanese National Character Survey of 2013 (a survey performed every five years since 1953), 72% of people declared they did not have any personal religious faith. In 1993 the figure was 67%, in 1983 it was 68%, and in 1963 it was 69%. Similarly, another well-known study, the Japanese General Social Survey, found in 2015 that 68.6% of the population did not follow any religion.

Australia

Every five years Australians fill out a comprehensive census, which in 2016 had a response rate of 95.1%. The format of the regular religious affiliation question was changed that year so that "No Religion" was the first check-box option on the list of religious denominations; in the 2011 census and others prior, it was a separate tick box underneath the "Other – please specify" box, right at the bottom of the list. Having this option poorly defined and less well-positioned allowed for more creativity than accuracy and 65,000 Australians declared themselves as "Jedi" in 2011. There was a sharp drop-off in this response with the updated and improved 2016 census, as seen in the chart below, while the number of respondents declaring they had "No Religion" jumped to over 30% from 22% five years earlier.

RELIGIOUS AFFILIATIONS, 2011 AND 2016

Religious Affiliations	2011(a)		2016	
	Populations ('000)	Population (%)	Populations ('000)	Population (%)
Christian	13 149.3	61.1	12 201.6	52.1
Catholic	5 439.3	25.3	5 291.8	22.6
Anglican	3 679.9	17.1	3 101.2	13.3
Uniting Church	1 065.8	5.0	870.2	3.7
Presbyterian and Reformed	599.5	2.8	526.7	2.3
Eastern Orthodox	563.1	2.6	502.8	2.1
Other Christian	1 801.8	8.4	1 908.9	8.2
Other Religions	1 546.3	7.2	1 920.8	8.2
Islam	476.3	2.2	604.2	2.6
Buddhism	529.0	2.5	563.7	2.4
Hinduism	275.5	1.3	440.3	1.9
Sikhism	72.3	0.3	125.9	0.5
Judaism	97.3	0.5	91.0	0.4
Other	95.9	0.4	95.7	0.4
No Religion(b)	4 804.6	22.3	7 040.7	30.1
Australia(c)	**21 507.7**	**100**	**23 401.9**	**100**

(a) 2011 data has been calculated using the 2016 definitions.

(b) No religion includes secular beliefs (e.g. Atheism) and other spiritual beliefs (e.g. New Age).

(c) As religion was an optional question, the total for Australia will not equal the sum of the items above it.

Image 27

Turkey

Turkey has a predominantly Muslim population of 84 million people, making it the 17th most populous nation on Earth. The ruling AKP party, led by President Recep Tayyip Erdogan, has been attempting to turn Turkey into a more religious society, and Erdogan has declared his desire to "raise a pious generation" in line with his Islamist ideals. However, trends in religious adherence in the country are heading in the opposite direction, and under Erdogan's rule, while the government has become more religious, society has become less so. Furthermore, Turkey has quite a young population, with a median age of 32 (compared to 38 in the United States and 40 in the United Kingdom), so as young people become increasingly secularized, the proportion of the population abandoning religion will steadily increase. This is backed up by recent surveys, including the annual "Lifestyles Survey" conducted each year between 2008 and 2018 by Turkish research agency KONDA, which showed that in those ten years:

1. The proportion of young people who defined themselves as "pious conservative" dropped from 25% to 15%.
2. The proportion of young people who described themselves as religious dropped from 51% to 43%.
3. The proportion of young people who stated that they fast during Ramadan decreased from 74% to 58% (in the general population it dropped from 77% to 65%).
4. The proportion of people who regularly performed prayers decreased from 27% to 24%.
5. The level of young people who wore no headcover reached 58%, whereas in the general population it was 37%.
6. The proportion of people with high-school education has increased from 29% to 45%, while university attendance has increased from 16% to 22%.

The population is becoming more tolerant, as indicated by the proportion of respondents who say they would accept a son-in-law or daughter-in-law with different religious beliefs increasing from 47% to 64%.

Iran

Iran is an Islamic country of 82 million people, making it the world's 18th largest population. Its political system has elements of democracy; however, in real terms, it is run as an authoritarian theocracy.

In one of the most fascinating recent surveys and the most comprehensive in decades, 40,000 Iranians living in Iran were polled, revealing an extraordinary change in people's connection to religion. As the government in Iran would never allow such questions to be asked internally, the survey was conducted by a research company GAMAAN (Group for Analyzing and Measuring Attitudes in Iran) based in The Netherlands.

In Iran, people are still sentenced to death for apostasy, and punished for making or posting anti-religious comments – even for dancing in public. Given those threats hanging over Iranians' heads, it is impressive that the study released in August 2020 showed the following information:

Only 78% of the population believe in God – 22% don't or are unsure.

- Only 32% of the population consider themselves Shia Muslim (yet, officially, Shia Muslims constitute approximately 90% of the population). This suggests that although a relatively large percentage of Iranians believe in a deity, they do not subscribe to the Muslim religious view of it.
- 47% raised with religion no longer consider themselves religious.
- 37% of Iranians drink alcohol regularly or occasionally, despite its prohibition since the revolution in 1979, the difficulty in obtaining it, and its usually high price.
- Only 37% believe in life after death (a major tenet of Islam).
- Only 30% believe in heaven and hell.
- 60% don't participate in regular prayer rituals.
- 72% of the population disagree with the hijab being mandatory, and in response to a follow-up question 58% said they do not believe in the use of the hijab at all.
- 68% say that the laws of the country should not be based on religion.
- When asked if they agree with their children being taught religion in school, 56% said no, 27% said yes and 17% neither agreed nor disagreed.

Combining the None, Atheist, Agnostic and "Humanist" groups in the following pie chart suggests that 40% of the Iranian population are not religious. On top of that, many of the other groupings will contain a percentage of people who feel culturally and historically connected to a religion but are not particularly religious.

Which of the following is closer to your beliefs and faith?

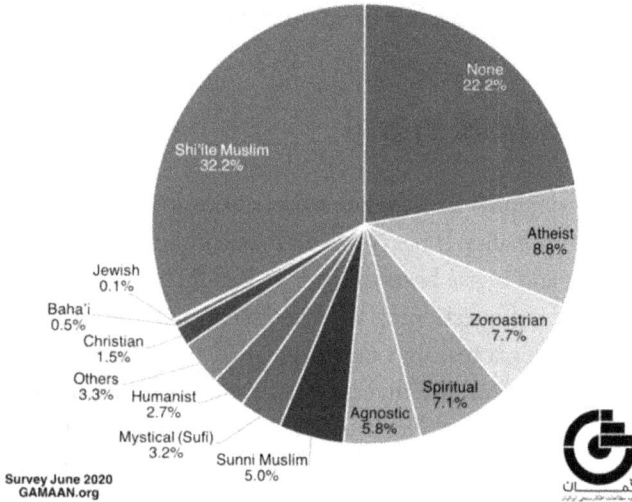

Image 28

The following chart shows how 46.8% of Iranians have, within their life-times, changed from "being religious to non-religious". That is an unbelievable change, and one that is, again, more pronounced in the younger generation, where 51.8% of 20–29-year-olds raised religious have become non-religious.

How have your religious (or non-religious) beliefs changed during your lifetime?

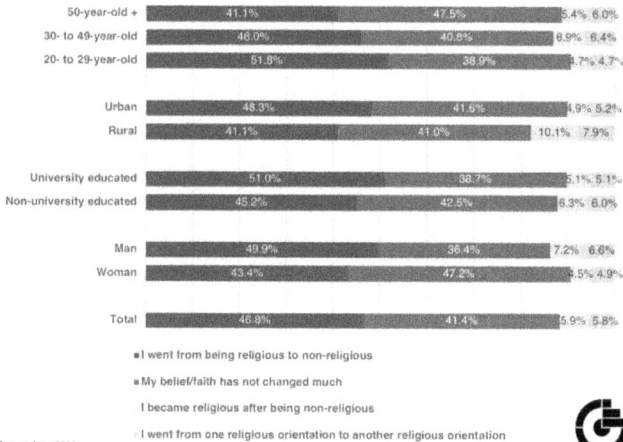

Image 29

It appears as though a similar situation to Turkey is occurring, whereby a minority theocratic leadership is holding its increasingly secular majority population hostage.

Trends in the Arab world

The Arab world is a region of disparate nationalities and cultures that still retain a substantive commonality. It has been somewhat closed off to the liberties that exist in the West and it has been difficult to conduct surveys there on beliefs, as the relevant lines of questioning are often seen as offensive or blasphemous.

In 2006, however, a research network called Arab Barometer was set up. Operating out of Princeton University, it aims to conduct high-quality surveys in the Middle East and North Africa. To date more than 70,000 people have been interviewed in 15 countries. The most recent "fifth-wave" survey from 2018–19 included results from 25,407 people in ten countries plus the Palestinian Territories. The data shows a rapid increase in secularism in the five years since the previous survey.

Rise of the non-religious

Proportion of people who said they were not religious in 2013 and 2018-19

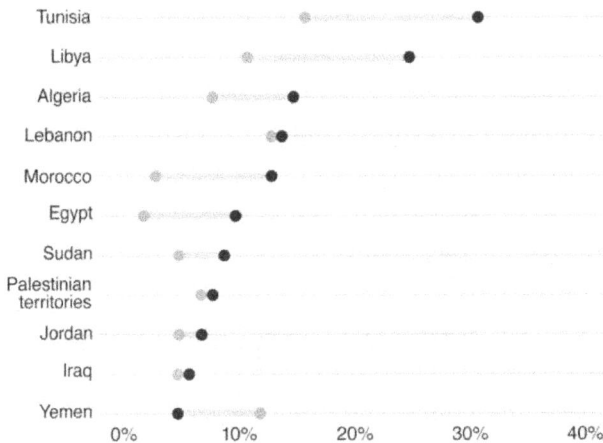

Source: Arab Barometer   BBC

Since 2013, the number of people across the region identifying as "not religious" has risen from 8% to 13%. The rise is greatest in the under 30s, among whom 18% identify as not religious, according to the research. Only Yemen saw a fall in the category.

Image 30

Back in 2013, around 14% of Tunisians said they were non-religious but that rose to 31% in 2019. In Libya the figure has jumped from 11% to 25% in Morocco from 4% to 13%, and in Egypt, which has strong anti-blasphemy and anti-atheism laws, there has been a sharp rise, from 3% to 10%.

Even in the face of prosecution, imprisonment and ostracism, more and more people in the Arab world are defining themselves as non-religious. Many of them are young people, with the survey data finding that among those under 30, 18% define themselves as non-religious, up from 11% in five years. In fact, if you drill deeper into the data, you find that young Tunisians (46%) are just as likely to say they are not religious as young Americans (45%)!

This translates to tens of millions of contemporary Arabs connecting more with secularity than a religious way of life in the last five years alone. The future influence of this will be significant, as non-religious adults usually beget non-religious children (whereas people raised in non-religious families do not often become religious).

According to another part of the survey, two-thirds of young people believe that religion is too influential in the Middle East, eight in ten believe that religious institutions require reform, and a majority support the idea of female prime ministers or presidents. It appears that views on whether Islam is compatible with democracy are changing quite rapidly, and that the kind of religion that endures will be a more secular/cultural version of Islam.

This could have significant knock-on effects because if religion plays a lesser role in these societies, then we can expect changes to the politics of the region. Only this year, the UAE, Bahrain and Sudan announced peace accords with Israel, and a few other Arabic countries have indicated that they may soon follow suit. It appears that increasing secularism may be the key to finally achieving peace in the Middle East. We may be on the cusp of major changes here.

The tide is also turning against religious political parties, religious leaders and attendance at mosque services. The "Arab Spring" of less than a decade ago was a series of uprisings across the region against oppressive regimes, which led to a number of rulers being deposed. Many of those regimes had been strongly influenced by Islamist thought and some of the goals of the demonstrations included more democratic systems, increased human rights and freedoms and greater secularism.

Overall, trust in Islamist parties fell dramatically across the region from 35% in 2013 to 20% only five years later (Image 31). It is evident that the secularization being seen in the West is also happening across the Arab world.

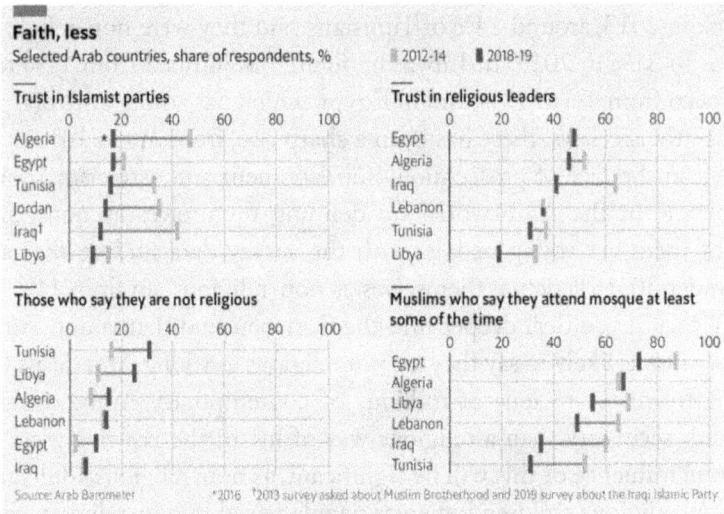

Faith, less
Selected Arab countries, share of respondents, %   ▌2012-14 ▌2018-19

Image 31

There is still, however, acceptance of some religious dogma in many Arab states, including some highly objectionable practices. Honour killings, for instance, are in some countries considered acceptable by a significant percentage of the population, while homosexuality is still not.

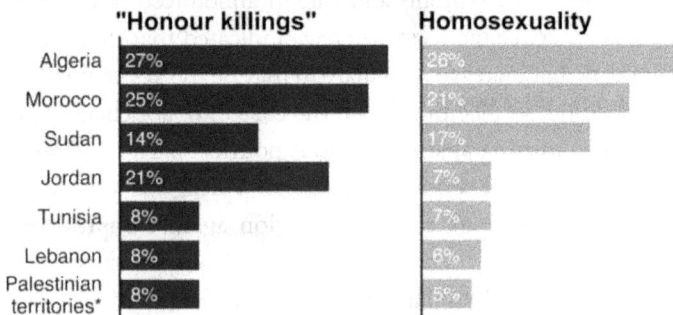

"Honour killing" more acceptable than homosexuality

Proportion of respondents considering the below acceptable

	"Honour killings"	Homosexuality
Algeria	27%	26%
Morocco	25%	21%
Sudan	14%	17%
Jordan	21%	7%
Tunisia	8%	7%
Lebanon	8%	6%
Palestinian territories*	8%	5%

Respondents identified acceptable practices from a list.
*Data contains only responses from the West Bank

Source: Arab Barometer   B B C

Image 32

Across the globe

Pew Research has also conducted global surveys. The following is the part of the introduction to their article "The Age Gap in Religion Across the World", published in June 2018:

> In the United States, religious congregations have been graying for decades, and young adults are now much less religious than their elders. Recent surveys have found that younger adults are far less likely than older generations to identify with a religion, believe in God or engage in a variety of religious practices.
>
> But this is not solely an American phenomenon: Lower religious observance among younger adults is common around the world, according to a new analysis of Pew Research Center surveys conducted in more than 100 countries and territories over the last decade.
>
> Although the age gap in religious commitment is larger in some nations than in others, it occurs in many different economic and social contexts – in developing countries as well as advanced industrial economies, in Muslim-majority nations as well as predominantly Christian states, and in societies that are, overall, highly religious as well as those that are comparatively secular.[7]

In 2012, WIN-Gallup International, a network of the world's top independent pollsters, conducted a survey of 57 countries across the globe, questioning more than 50,000 people, entitled "Global Index of Religiosity and Atheism". The main question asked was: "Irrespective of whether you attend a place of worship or not, would you say you are a religious person, not a religious person or a convinced atheist?"; there was also a fourth possible answer: "Don't know/no response".

The results, as the following table shows, included the finding that 36% of people worldwide describe themselves as either not religious or a convinced atheist.

Global Average*	51927	59%	23%	13%	5%

Countries in alphabetical order	Sample size	A religious person	Not a religious person	A convinced athiest	Don't know / no response
Afghanistan	1031	83%	15%	0%	2%
Argentina	1002	72%	19%	7%	1%
Armenia	500	92%	3%	2%	2%
Australia	1040	37%	48%	10%	5%
Austria	1003	42%	43%	10%	5%
Azerbaijan	510	44%	51%	0%	5%
Belgium	528	59%	26%	8%	7%
Bosnia and Herzegovina	1000	67%	25%	4%	4%
Brazil	2002	85%	13%	1%	1%
Bulgaria	997	59%	28%	2%	12%
Cameroon	504	82%	14%	3%	1%
Canada	1003	46%	40%	9%	5%
China	500	14%	30%	47%	9%
Colombia	606	83%	12%	3%	2%
Czech Republic	1000	20%	48%	30%	2%
Ecuador	400	70%	27%	2%	2%
Fiji	1020	92%	5%	1%	2%
Finland	984	53%	38%	6%	3%
France	1671	37%	34%	29%	1%
Georgia	1000	84%	12%	1%	3%
Germany	502	51%	33%	15%	1%
Ghana	1505	96%	2%	0%	1%
Hong Kong	500	38%	51%	9%	2%
Iceland	852	57%	31%	10%	2%
India	1091	81%	13%	3%	3%
Iraq	1000	88%	9%	0%	3%
Ireland	1001	47%	44%	10%	0%
Italy	987	73%	15%	8%	4%

Japan	1200	16%	31%	31%	23%
Kenya	1000	88%	9%	2%	1%
Korea, Rep (South)	1524	52%	31%	15%	2%
Lebanon	500	64%	33%	2%	2%
Lithuania	1025	69%	22%	1%	7%
Macedonia	1209	90%	8%	1%	1%
Malaysia	520	81%	13%	0%	6%
Moldova	1086	83%	5%	5%	7%
Netherlands	505	43%	42%	14%	2%
Nigeria	1049	93%	4%	1%	2%
Pakistan	2705	84%	8%	2%	6%
Palestinian territories (West Bank and Gaza)	626	65%	29%	4%	2%
Peru	1207	86%	8%	3%	3%
Poland	520	81%	9%	5%	6%
Romania	1050	89%	6%	1%	3%
Russian Federation	1000	55%	26%	6%	13%
Saudi Arabia	502	75%	19%	5%	1%
Serbia	1037	77%	16%	3%	4%
South Africa	200	64%	28%	4%	5%
South Sudan	1020	79%	10%	6%	5%
Spain	1146	52%	38%	9%	1%
Sweden	501	29%	50%	8%	12%
Switzerland	507	50%	38%	9%	4%
Tunisia	503	75%	22%	0%	2%
Turkey	1031	23%	73%	2%	2%
Ukraine	1013	71%	20%	3%	6%
United States	1002	60%	30%	5%	5%
Uzbekistan	500	79%	16%	2%	3%
Vietnam	500	30%	65%	0%	5%

Image 33

Let's look a bit deeper into some of these statistics, as the figures for countries that apparently have zero "convinced atheists" are unlikely to be accurate. Every country polled that has no atheists is a Muslim country, apart from Vietnam. There are inherent difficulties in assessing such issues in strongly Islamic countries, as apostasy laws and community pressures make it almost impossible for respondents to publicly state that they are convinced atheists.

A good example of this is Azerbaijan, which was under the control of Soviet atheist policies for many decades and is considered one of the most secular Muslim countries in the world. The US Department of State 2019 "Report on International Religious Freedom: Azerbaijan" summarizes the situation thus: "The constitution stipulates the separation of state and religion and the equality of all religions and all individuals regardless of belief. It protects freedom of religion, including the right of individuals to profess, individually or together with others, any religion, or to profess no religion, and to express and spread religious belief."[8] Given that the country was controlled by the Soviet regime for so long, it seems doubtful that there are zero "convinced atheists" in Azerbaijan. Muslim identity is often based more on culture and ethnicity than actual religious practices.

In 2017, Pew Research released a study called "Muslims and Islam: Key Findings in the US and Around the World"[9] and one of the questions was about whether Sharia law should become the official law of the respondent's country. While the numbers in support of this were very high in countries like Afghanistan (99%), Iraq (91%), Malaysia (86%) and Tunisia (56%), they were notably low in the secular Muslim countries of Turkey (12%), Kazakhstan (10%) and Azerbaijan (8%). Therefore, having Azerbaijan on a par with the likes of Malaysia and Tunisia, as per Image 31, is not likely an accurate representation of where Azerbaijani Muslims reside on the spectrum. There are undoubtedly many more atheists and non-religious people in Muslim countries than most surveys show.

Support for Sharia

% of Muslims who favor making sharia the official law in their country

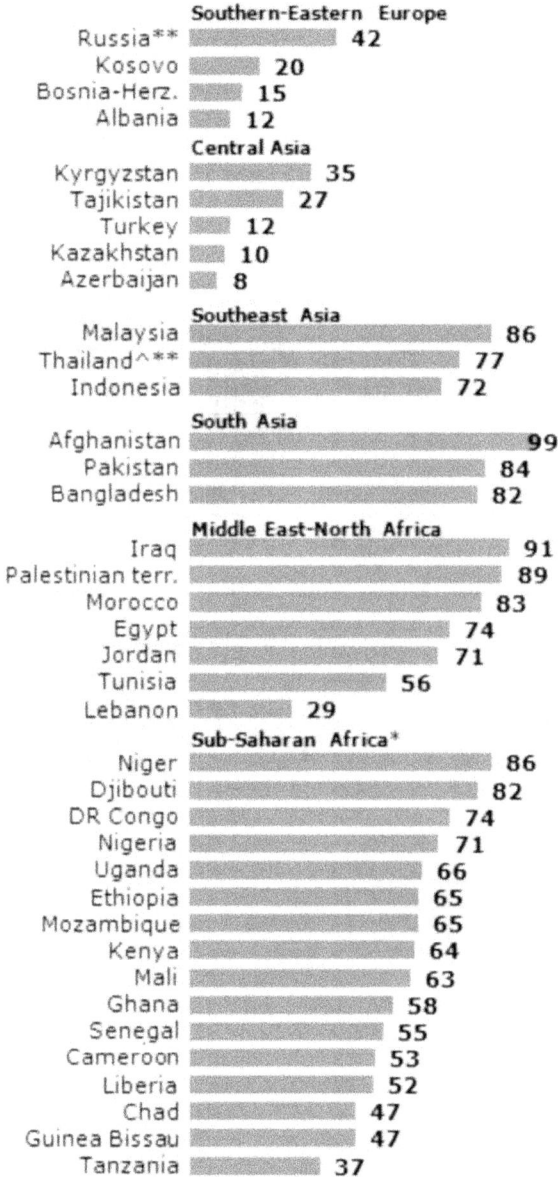

Southern-Eastern Europe

- Russia** — 42
- Kosovo — 20
- Bosnia-Herz. — 15
- Albania — 12

Central Asia

- Kyrgyzstan — 35
- Tajikistan — 27
- Turkey — 12
- Kazakhstan — 10
- Azerbaijan — 8

Southeast Asia

- Malaysia — 86
- Thailand^** — 77
- Indonesia — 72

South Asia

- Afghanistan — 99
- Pakistan — 84
- Bangladesh — 82

Middle East-North Africa

- Iraq — 91
- Palestinian terr. — 89
- Morocco — 83
- Egypt — 74
- Jordan — 71
- Tunisia — 56
- Lebanon — 29

Sub-Saharan Africa*

- Niger — 86
- Djibouti — 82
- DR Congo — 74
- Nigeria — 71
- Uganda — 66
- Ethiopia — 65
- Mozambique — 65
- Kenya — 64
- Mali — 63
- Ghana — 58
- Senegal — 55
- Cameroon — 53
- Liberia — 52
- Chad — 47
- Guinea Bissau — 47
- Tanzania — 37

Image 34

When countries are reassembled into regions, there is a considerable variation in beliefs in different parts of the globe. Latin America, a predominantly Catholic region, has a high affiliation with religion, as do Africa and South Asia. In contrast, there are low levels of affiliation in North Asia (where China predominates as a very atheistic society) and East Asia (skewed predominantly by Japan and South Korea). The other regions lie somewhere in between.

REGIONAL CLASSIFICATION					
	Sample Size Unweighted N	A religious person	Not a religious person	A convinced atheist	Don't know / no response
All Regions	**51927**	**59%**	**23%**	**13%**	**5%**
North America	2005	57%	33%	6%	5%
Latin America	5217	84%	13%	2%	1%
Western Europe	11227	51%	32%	14%	3%
Eastern Europe	12437	66%	21%	5%	8%
Africa	5278	89%	7%	2%	2%
Arab World	3131	77%	18%	2%	2%
West Asia	5777	64%	30%	3%	4%
South Asia	1091	83%	11%	3%	3%
East Asia	1020	39%	57%	0%	4%
North Asia	4744	17%	30%	42%	11%

Image 35

Of the 57 countries surveyed by WIN-Gallup International in 2012, 39 countries had been surveyed with the same question in 2005. In just those seven short years there was a highly significant global change, though with variation from country to country. Globally in that time period, there was a 9% drop in religiosity.

TREND IN RELIGIOSITY INDEX AMONG
39 COUNTRIES SURVEYED IN BOTH WAVES
(2005 - 2012)

Country (Rank order by 2012, High to low)	2005	2012	% change in Religiosity
Global Average	77%	68%	-9%
Ghana	96%	96%	0%
Nigeria	94%	93%	-1%
Macedonia	85%	90%	5%
Romania	85%	89%	4%
Kenya	89%	88%	-1%
Peru	84%	86%	2%
Pakistan	78%	84%	6%
Moldova	78%	83%	5%
Colombia	83%	83%	0%
Cameroon	86%	82%	-4%
Malaysia	77%	81%	4%
India	87%	81%	-6%
Poland	85%	81%	-4%
Serbia	72%	77%	5%
Italy	72%	73%	1%
Argentina	80%	72%	-8%
Ukraine	70%	71%	1%
Ecuador	85%	70%	-15%
Lithuania	75%	69%	-6%
Bosnia and Herzegovina	74%	67%	-7%
South Africa	83%	64%	-19%
United States	73%	60%	-13%
Bulgaria	63%	59%	-4%
Iceland	74%	57%	-17%
Russian Federation	57%	55%	-2%
Finland	51%	53%	2%
Korea, Rep (South)	58%	52%	-6%
Spain	55%	52%	-3%
Germany	60%	51%	-9%
Switzerland	71%	50%	-21%
Canada	58%	46%	-12%
Netherlands	42%	43%	1%
Austria	52%	42%	-10%
Hong Kong	-	-	-
France	58%	37%	-21%
Vietnam	53%	30%	-23%
Turkey	-	-	-
Czech Republic	22%	20%	-2%
Japan	17%	16%	-1%

Image 36

On top of this, there was also a massive shift globally in those who profess to being "convinced atheists", with the figure almost doubling across the 39 countries.

TRENDS IN ATHEISM INDEX AMONG
39 COUNTRIES SURVEYED IN BOTH WAVES
(2005 - 2012)

Country (Rank order by 2012, High to low)	2005	2012	% change in Atheism
Global Average	4%	7%	3%
Japan	23%	31%	8%
Czech Republic	20%	30%	10%
France	14%	29%	15%
Korea, Rep (South)	11%	15%	4%
Germany	10%	15%	5%
Netherlands	7%	14%	7%
Austria	10%	10%	0%
Iceland	6%	10%	4%
Canada	6%	9%	3%
Spain	10%	9%	-1%
Switzerland	7%	9%	2%
Hong Kong	-	-	-
Italy	6%	8%	2%
Argentina	2%	7%	5%
Russian Federation	4%	6%	2%
Finland	7%	6%	-1%
Moldova	2%	5%	3%
United States	1%	5%	4%
Poland	2%	5%	3%
South Africa	1%	4%	3%
Bosnia and Herzegovina	9%	4%	-5%
Ukraine	4%	3%	-1%
Colombia	3%	3%	0%
Cameroon	5%	3%	-2%
India	4%	3%	-1%
Peru	2%	3%	1%
Serbia	4%	3%	-1%
Bulgaria	5%	2%	-3%
Pakistan	1%	2%	1%
Ecuador	1%	2%	1%
Kenya	0%	2%	2%
Turkey	-	-	-
Lithuania	2%	1%	-1%
Romania	1%	1%	0%
Macedonia	3%	1%	-2%
Nigeria	1%	1%	0%
Malaysia	4%	0%	-4%
Ghana	0%	0%	0%
Vietnam	1%	0%	-1%

Image 37

A note was included in the study to explain why the data for both Turkey and Hong Kong was not included: "Both Turkey and Hong Kong show noticeable change since 2005. These changes are not from a faith to atheism but a shift from self-description of being 'Religious' to 'Not Religious'. We have requested researchers in both countries to investigate reasons which might explain this extraordinary shift."

Global trends in religious attendance

The chart below shows that in recent times the younger generations of both Christians and Muslims across the globe are on average attending religious services less frequently than those in the 40-plus age group.

Both Christians, Muslims show age gap in attendance

In the average country surveyed, % of adults who say they attend religious services at least weekly, among those who are ...

Religion	Ages 18-39	Ages 40+	% point difference Younger less religious ◄
All	36%	42%	6 pts.
Muslims	55	61	6
Christians	36	41	5
Unaffiliated	1	1	0

Note: Black bars indicate a difference greater than 5 percentage points. Differences are calculated based on unrounded numbers. Hindus, Buddhists and Jews are not shown because data on these groups are only available for a small number of countries.
Source: Pew Research Center surveys, 2008-2017.
"The Age Gap in Religion Around the World"

PEW RESEARCH CENTER

Image 38

One only has to look however at how many "ex-Muslim" groups now exist online across the globe to see that this change is often happening behind the anonymity of social media. For example, the following groups exist:

- On Facebook: Ex-Muslims' discussion group, Ex Muslims v Muslims, Muslims for Secular Democracy, Liberal Muslims United, American Council of Ex-Muslims ...
- On Twitter: Ex-Muslims' forum, Council of Ex-Muslims, Ex-Muslims of North America, Alliance of Former Muslims, Ex-Muslims of Scandinavia, ExMuslimNews.org ...

The Richard Dawkins Foundation announced in 2018 that there had been at least 13 million downloads of unofficial Arabic PDFs of Dawkins' book *The God Delusion*, including 3 million copies in Saudi Arabia alone.[10] Because of this, the foundation has organized for the book and a number of Dawkins' other bestsellers to be translated into Urdu, Farsi, Indonesian and other Islamic languages, for free download. Education and knowledge are recognized as key drivers of the shift to secularism and the Richard Dawkins Foundation is doing its utmost to support this change.

The importance of religion among the young

Across the globe among the young, the trend towards secularism mimics the changes in Western countries, and it's clear that religion is significantly less important to younger generations than it is to older people, as shown in this chart.

Among Christians, 7-point age gap in share who say religion is very important

In the average country surveyed, % of adults who say religion is very important in their lives, among those who are ...

Religion	Ages 18-39	Ages 40+	% point difference Younger less religious ◄
All	51%	57%	6 pts.
Christians	50	56	7
Muslims	76	79	3
Unaffiliated	3	4	1

Note: Black bars indicate a difference greater than 5 percentage points. Differences are calculated based on unrounded numbers. Hindus, Buddhists and Jews are not shown because data on these groups are only available for a small number of countries.
Source: Pew Research Center Surveys, 2008-2017.
"The Age Gap in Religion Around the World"

PEW RESEARCH CENTER

Image 39

Echoing the earlier graph that showed reduced attendance at religious services in the United States (Image 4), the graph below shows that, across the globe generally, young people are invariably turning away from regular prayer rituals.

Double-digit gaps in daily prayer in several regions

In the average country surveyed, % of adults who pray daily, among those living in ...

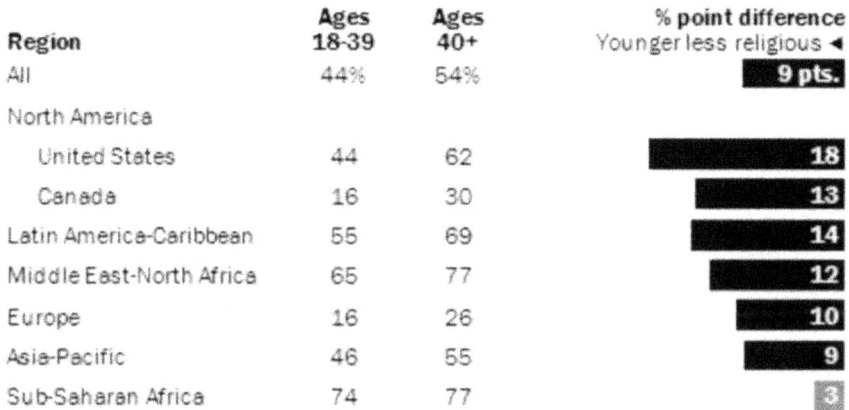

Region	Ages 18-39	Ages 40+	% point difference Younger less religious ◄
All	44%	54%	9 pts.
North America			
United States	44	62	18
Canada	16	30	13
Latin America-Caribbean	55	69	14
Middle East-North Africa	65	77	12
Europe	16	26	10
Asia-Pacific	46	55	9
Sub-Saharan Africa	74	77	3

Image 40

As shown in the charts below, it is also true that, generally, younger people worldwide are becoming less religious than the older generations. This matches up with the data shown in Images 4, 5 and 6 for the United States.

Younger adults are rarely more religious than older adults, regardless of faith

Number of countries with each outcome, by religion

	Religion less important to younger adults	Religion less important to older adults	No significant difference
Overall	46	2	58
Christians	37	1	40
Muslims	10	0	32
Unaffiliated	8	2	19
Hindus	0	0	2
Buddhists	1	0	4
Jews	0	0	2

Note: Younger adults are those ages 18 to 39; older adults are those 40 and older.
Source: Pew Research Center surveys, 2008-2017.
"The Age Gap in Religion Around the World"

PEW RESEARCH CENTER

Image 41

Younger adults are less likely to identify with a religion in North America, Europe and Latin America

In the average country surveyed, % of adults who are affiliated with a religious group, among those living in ...

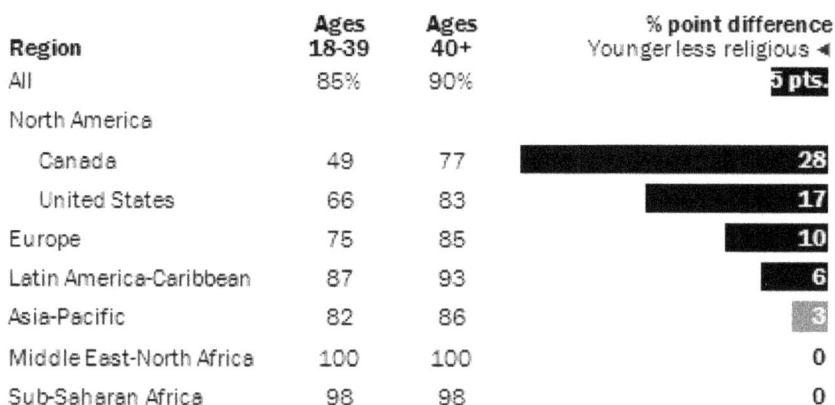

Region	Ages 18-39	Ages 40+	% point difference Younger less religious ◄
All	85%	90%	5 pts.
North America			
Canada	49	77	28
United States	66	83	17
Europe	75	85	10
Latin America-Caribbean	87	93	6
Asia-Pacific	82	86	3
Middle East-North Africa	100	100	0
Sub-Saharan Africa	98	98	0

Note: Black bars indicate a difference greater than 5 percentage points. Differences are calculated based on unrounded numbers.
Source: Pew Research Center surveys, 2008-2017.
"The Age Gap in Religion Around the World"

PEW RESEARCH CENTER

Image 42

The extent of the change varies from place to place and, again, data emanating from Muslim countries is likely to be skewed due to people being fearful of publicly renouncing religion. This is possibly why in the above chart there is a 100% affiliation with religion in the Middle East–North Africa region and a 98% affiliation in Sub-Saharan Africa.

When we look at global statistics, as in the chart below, we find, again, that in nearly every country across the globe, the younger generations are less religious than the older generations. This is observed in Christian majority countries, Muslim majority countries and even in countries where the majority of people have no religious affiliation.

In Poland, 45 other countries, young adults less likely to say religion very important in their lives

Percentage-point differences in shares of younger (ages 18-39) and older adults (ages 40+) who consider religion very important

Largest religious group in country

● Christians

▲ Muslims

■ Unaffiliated

In 46 countries, younger adults are less likely to consider religion "very important" than older adults.

Younger less religious ◄ | ► Older less re

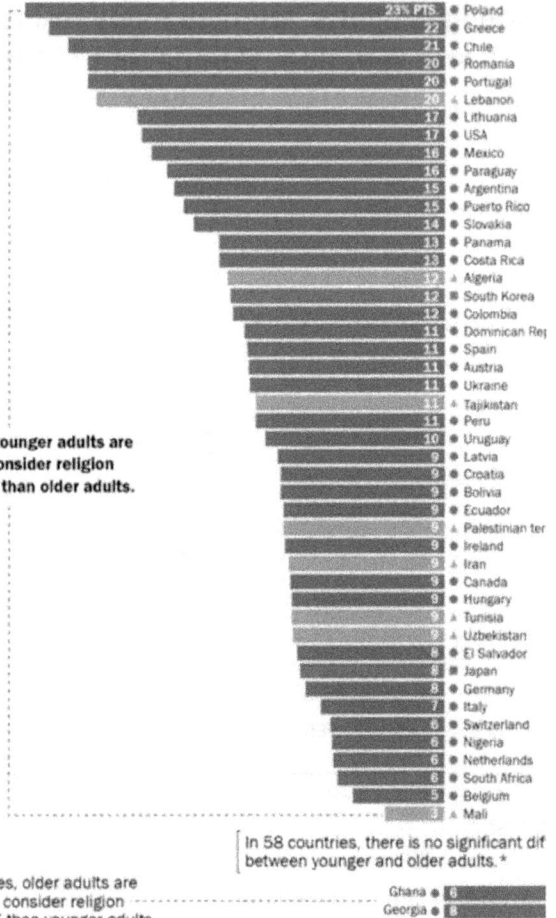

Pts		Country
23% PTS.	●	Poland
22	●	Greece
21	●	Chile
20	●	Romania
20	●	Portugal
20	▲	Lebanon
17	●	Lithuania
17	●	USA
16	●	Mexico
16	●	Paraguay
15	●	Argentina
15	●	Puerto Rico
14	●	Slovakia
13	●	Panama
13	●	Costa Rica
12	▲	Algeria
12	■	South Korea
12	●	Colombia
11	●	Dominican Rep
11	●	Spain
11	●	Austria
11	●	Ukraine
11	▲	Tajikistan
11	●	Peru
10	●	Uruguay
9	●	Latvia
9	●	Croatia
9	●	Bolivia
9	●	Ecuador
9	▲	Palestinian ter
9	●	Ireland
9	▲	Iran
9	●	Canada
9	●	Hungary
	▲	Tunisia
	▲	Uzbekistan
8	●	El Salvador
8	■	Japan
8	●	Germany
7	●	Italy
6	●	Switzerland
6	●	Nigeria
6	●	Netherlands
6	●	South Africa
5	●	Belgium
3	▲	Mali

In 58 countries, there is no significant dif between younger and older adults. *

In two countries, older adults are less likely to consider religion "very important" than younger adults.

Ghana ● ■
Georgia ● ■

Image 43

In the chart below, the three countries where young people attend religious services more frequently than their older counterparts are all countries that experienced wars while the younger generation were traversing their adolescent period.

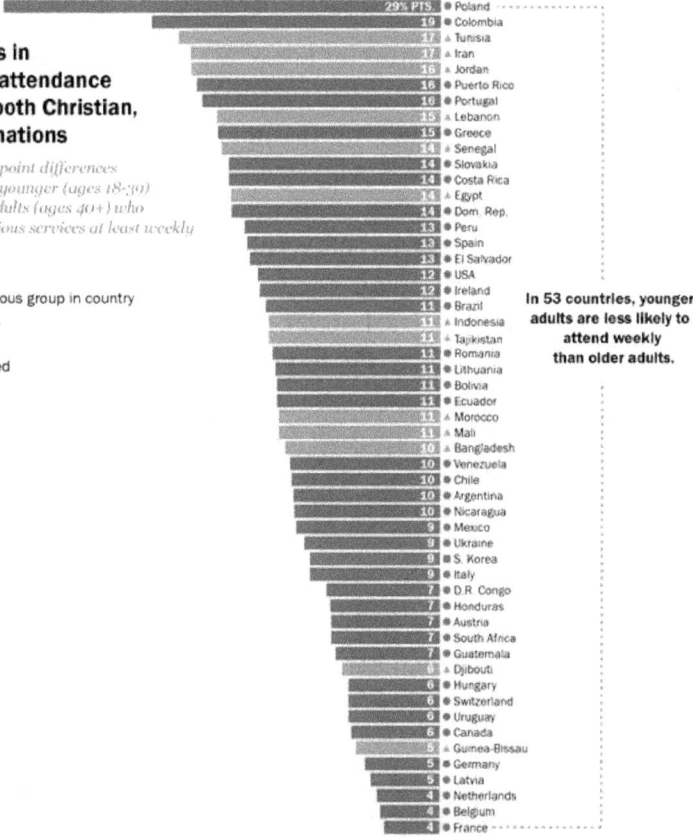

Age gaps in worship attendance seen in both Christian, Muslim nations

Percentage-point differences in shares of younger (ages 18-39) and older adults (ages 40+) who attend religious services at least weekly

Largest religious group in country
● Christians
▲ Muslims
▓ Unaffiliated

Younger attend less ◄ | ► Older attend less

29% PTS.	● Poland
19	● Colombia
17	▲ Tunisia
17	▲ Iran
16	▲ Jordan
16	● Puerto Rico
16	● Portugal
15	▲ Lebanon
15	● Greece
14	● Senegal
14	● Slovakia
14	● Costa Rica
14	▲ Egypt
14	● Dom. Rep.
13	● Peru
13	● Spain
13	● El Salvador
12	● USA
12	● Ireland
11	● Brazil
11	▲ Indonesia
11	▲ Tajikistan
11	● Romania
11	● Lithuania
11	● Bolivia
11	● Ecuador
11	▲ Morocco
11	▲ Mali
10	▲ Bangladesh
10	● Venezuela
10	● Chile
10	● Argentina
10	● Nicaragua
9	● Mexico
9	● Ukraine
9	▓ S. Korea
9	● Italy
7	● D.R. Congo
7	● Honduras
7	● Austria
7	● South Africa
7	● Guatemala
6	▲ Djibouti
6	● Hungary
6	● Switzerland
6	● Uruguay
6	● Canada
5	▲ Guinea-Bissau
5	● Germany
5	● Latvia
4	● Netherlands
4	● Belgium
4	● France

In 53 countries, younger adults are less likely to attend weekly than older adults.

[In 46 countries, there is no significant difference between younger and older adults.*]

In three countries, older adults are less likely to attend weekly than younger adults.

Armenia ●	4
Rwanda ●	9
Liberia ●	19

*These include the following countries. Christians are largest religious group: Australia, Belarus, Bosnia-Herzegovina, Botswana, Bulgaria, Cameroon, Croatia, Denmark, Ethiopia, Finland, Georgia, Ghana, Kenya, Moldova, Mozambique, Nigeria, Norway, Panama, Paraguay, the Philippines, Russia, Serbia, Sweden, Tanzania, Uganda, United Kingdom and Zambia. Muslims are largest religious group: Afghanistan, Albania, Algeria, Azerbaijan, Chad, Iraq, Kazakhstan, Kosovo, Kyrgyzstan, Malaysia, Niger, Pakistan, Palestinian territories, Turkey and Uzbekistan. Unaffiliated are largest religious group: China, Czech Republic and Estonia.

Source: Pew Research Center surveys, 2008-2017.
"The Age Gap in Religion Around the World"

PEW RESEARCH CENTER

Image 44

Like the big tobacco companies, religions have been forced to focus more on the developing world in recent decades – as education enlightens on the respective dangers of both!

The influence of wealth

What influence does wealth have on belief in a god, frequency of involvement in prayer and sources of moral guidance? A number of studies have shown a correlation between level of education and secularization. Increased exposure to information outside religion allows people to hear other ideas and gain a broader understanding of science and other cultures, as well as a new perspective on how a religion sits within the greater global context, and in turn how likely it is to be "true".

A WIN-Gallup International survey from 2012 assessed religiosity versus income/prosperity as well as education levels within 57 countries. Within each country surveyed, the population was divided into five groups: Bottom Quintile (low income), Medium-Low Quintile, Medium Quintile, Medium-High Quintile and High Quintile. It was found that there was a continually decreasing percentage of people describing themselves as religious as income increased.[11]

Bottom Quintile (low income)	66%
Medium-Low Quintile	65%
Medium Quintile	56%
Medium-High Quintile	51%
High Quintile (high income)	49%

A similar trend was seen in Pew Research's "Landscape Study" in the United States (Image 45), with double the number of people in the highest income bracket responding "Do not believe in God" compared to the same category in the lowest income bracket (14% v. 7%). Considering that we are all the same species, this suggests that financial security has a very strong effect on one's belief in a deity.

Belief in God by household income (2014)

% of adults who say they...

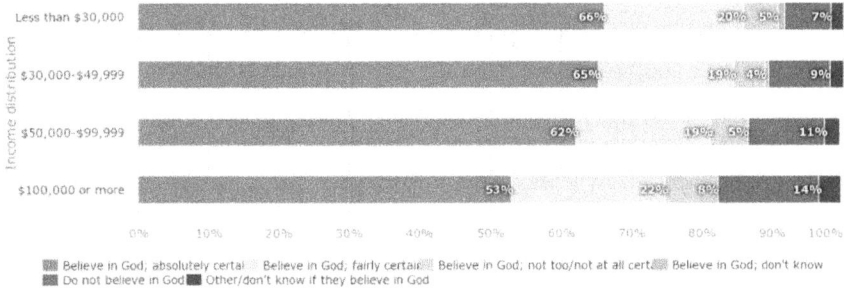

Image 45

Similarly, Pew Research's "Global Attitudes" report showed a correlation between increasing wealth of a country and the declining importance of religion.

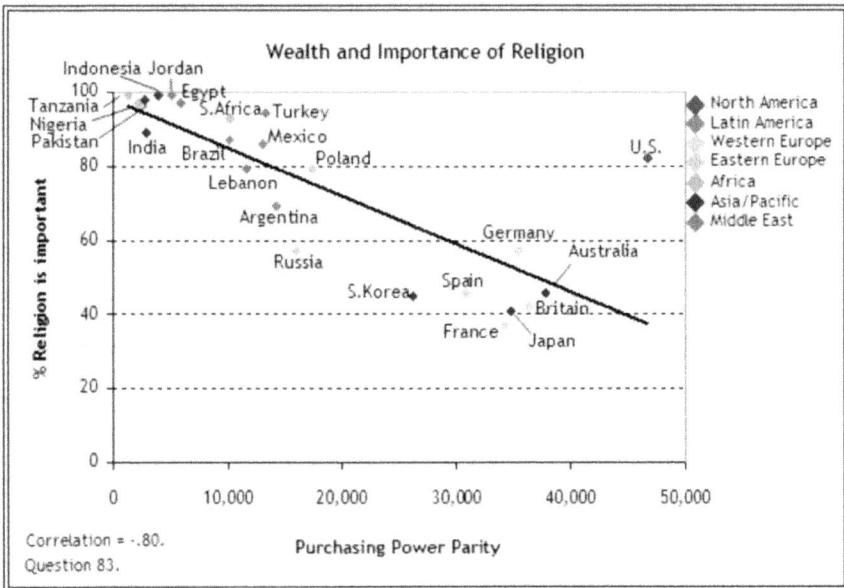

Image 46

The influence of education

Education levels are often a predictor of one's beliefs on a range of topics and also affect people's views on religion. Generally, as the level of education increases, levels of religiosity decline.

The WIN-Gallup 2012 study was able to also use its data to assess, at an international level, how level of education affects religious adherence. When looking at those people who defined themselves as religious, the results were:

Less than secondary education	68%
Secondary education	61%
Higher education	52%

Pew Research has also assessed the relationship between level of education and association with religious practices and beliefs in the United States. If you are an American with a postgraduate degree, you are approximately two and a half times more likely to be an atheist than someone who has only a high-school education or less.

Belief in God by educational group (2014)

% of adults who say they...

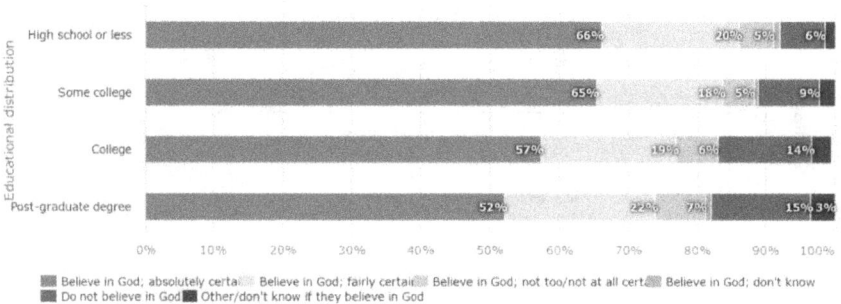

Educational distribution				
High school or less	66%	20%	5%	6%
Some college	65%	16%	5%	9%
College	57%	19%	6%	14%
Post-graduate degree	52%	22%	7%	15% 3%

Believe in God; absolutely certain　Believe in God; fairly certain　Believe in God; not too/not at all certain　Believe in God; don't know
Do not believe in God　Other/don't know if they believe in God

PEW RESEARCH CENTER

Image 47

Education level also affects the kind of deity people believe in, whether it be the god described in the Bible or a less specific deity that simply constitutes a higher force than us. Again, those with a high-school education or less are approximately 50% more likely to believe in the God of the Bible than someone who is a college graduate.

College graduates less likely to believe in active, involved deity

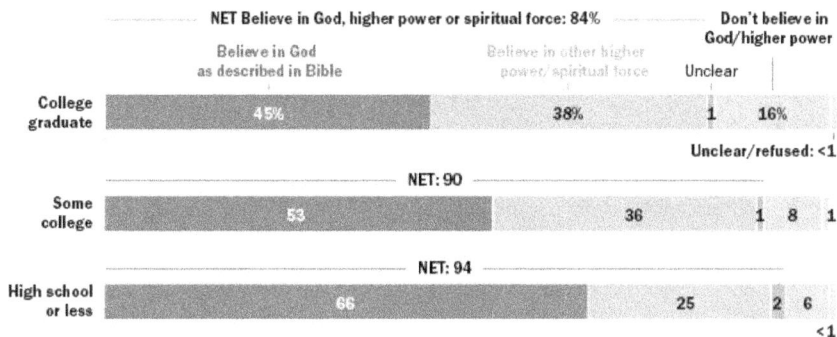

Image 48

Similar effects are likely to become evident across both the Muslim and Hindu worlds. There will likely be a slight lag compared to developed nations, but as the world continues to become more educated and greater numbers of children complete high school as well as university degrees and are exposed to information from outside their traditional upbringing, we will inevitably see increasing secularism in these regions too.

The following graph shows a rapid increase in the percentage of people attending some form of school in Muslim and Hindu communities. On top of this, the average number of years of schooling is increasing among these two religious groups.

Muslims and Hindus have made the largest gains in shares with at least some schooling

% of each generation with any formal schooling, by religious group

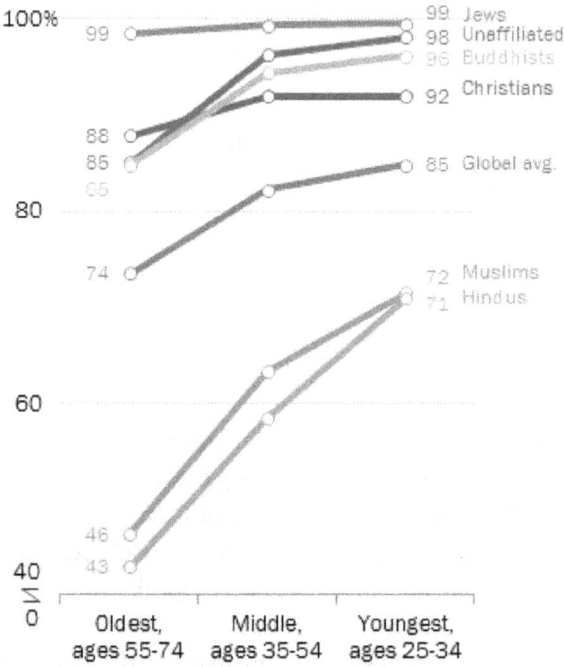

Note: The oldest, middle and youngest cohorts were born 1936-1955, 1956-1975 and 1976-1985, respectively, and were ages 55-74, 35-54 and 25-34 as of 2010.
Source: Pew Research Center analysis. See Methodology for more details.
"Religion and Education Around the World"

PEW RESEARCH CENTER

Image 49

It is heartening to see a substantial increase in education levels among all groups but especially those who are coming from a very low base. As Hindus and Muslims "catch up" with the rest of the world, there will likely be many positive flow-on effects aside from decreased religiosity, including the emancipation of women, the average age of first pregnancy rising, fewer children, increased ability to find employment opportunities, and so on.

Muslims and Hindus have made the largest gains in educational attainment over decades

Average years of formal schooling, by religious group across three generations

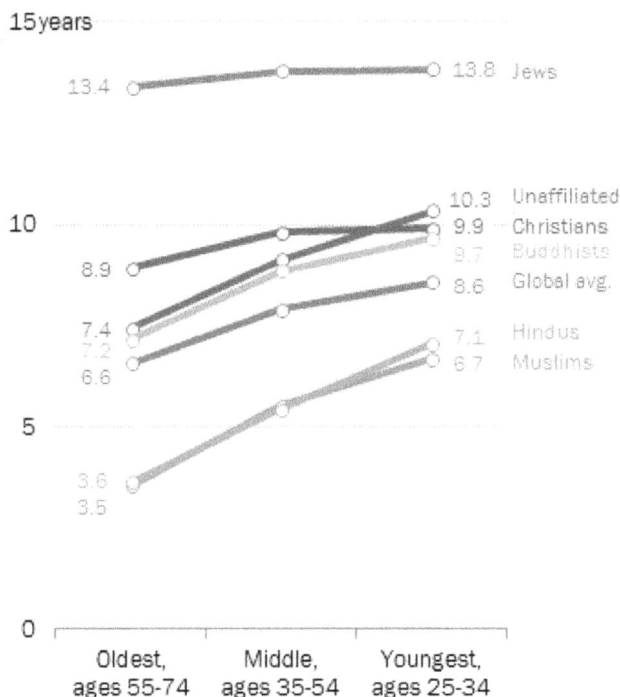

15 years

13.4 ○――――――○――――――○ 13.8 Jews

10

8.9 ○

7.4 ○
7.2
6.6 ○

10.3 Unaffiliated
9.9 Christians
9.7 Buddhists
8.6 Global avg.

7.1 Hindus
6.7 Muslims

5

3.6 ○
3.5

0

Oldest,	Middle,	Youngest,
ages 55-74	ages 35-54	ages 25-34

Note: The oldest, middle and youngest cohorts were born 1936-1955, 1956-1975 and 1976-1985, respectively, and were ages 55-74, 35-54 and 25-34 as of 2010.

Source: Pew Research Center analysis. See Methodology for more details. "Religion and Education Around the World"

PEW RESEARCH CENTER

Image 50

How religion affects one's worldview

The Biblical explanation of the origin of life has for millennia been that man was created "in God's image" and therefore we are the exceptional species on the planet. This notion has encouraged humans to feel justified in holding dominion over nature, even as many of us realize that we have to act responsibly in our treatment of other creatures. Of those who do not believe in a god, 77% say that stricter environmental laws are worth the economic cost, whereas only 51% of those who absolutely believe in a god agree with that statement. This suggests that a beneficial side-effect of the shift away from religion will be a stronger inclination to make tough decisions that will benefit the long-term health of our planet.

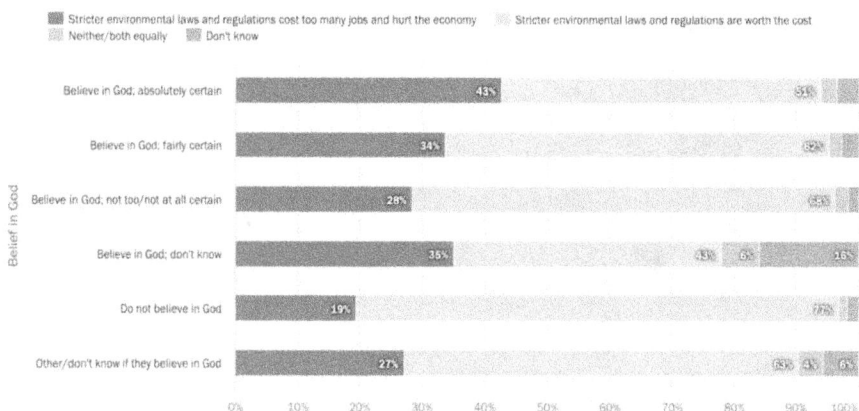

Image 51

Another study published in *Social Society Quarterly* (in November 2015) came to a similar conclusion: "… we find notable variation across and within these traditions. In particular, when we allow for possible differences within Protestantism, we find the negative association between being Protestant and environmental attitudes is particularly strong among Evangelicals … These findings suggest that individuals in religious traditions that are more prone to teach biblical literalism are less likely to express high degrees of concern about the environment."[12]

Conclusions

Many people who do not see themselves as religious remain happily coupled to their Christian/Jewish/Muslim/Hindu heritage. They find interest in or admire and relate to the stories of their religion, even if they don't believe them to be true events. They often wish to observe some of the festivals and values that are part of their religion and sed their children to faith schools, but they treat their religion more as a philosophical standpoint than as a deity-based dogma. They want to remain connected to the community that they have been raised in and continue some of its cultural practices. They see the religion that they have been raised in as a potential source of spiritual comfort but can also see the problems and falsehoods that exist within much of the dogma.

Across most nations and religions, young people especially are becoming less interested in and engaged by religious ceremonies, prayer rituals and prohibitive strictures, and fewer believe in the "overseeing deity in the sky" concept. A portmanteau word has recently been coined to describe their status: "apatheist", a combination of the words *apathy* and *theism*, referring to their perceived apathy and lack of interest in theism. These young people have moved past atheists (who are often actively engaged in the discourse) to a point where they feel the discussion doesn't even warrant their time or energy. For them, it's like discussing whether fairies are real.

Furthermore, an increasing number of people who wish to remain connected to the religion they were raised in and still cling to a deity concept redefine "Him" as a vague, asexual, supernatural source of good, love and charity – which are all in fact innate human characteristics. This must surely make their deity far less awe-inspiring and incline these people's practice of their religions more towards life-philosophies such as Buddhism. This is a further step in the right direction, whereby anyone can avail themselves of all potentially advantageous spiritual concepts. And one step closer to complete non-theism.

It appears certain that some religious groupings will be redefined in the coming decades as predominantly cultural practices, based on historical connections. Over time, these cultural practices will continue to blend and be shared by a wider variety of the populace. As we slowly return to being one civilization, the entire world will adopt more similar views. After all, when things really work, everyone begins to adopt them. And this is where an evidence-based outlook can be a unifying force.

These changes will be vastly different to the loss of religion that occurred last century in Communist countries and or even in Muslim countries like Iran (under Mohammad Reza Shah) and Turkey (under Mustafa Kemal Atatürk). Those situations occurred as a result of a "top-down" mechanism, whereby the state imposed changes rather than them being a genuine shift in people's mindsets. They were "enforced beliefs", which were never going to survive long-term. In contrast, the current changes are bottom-up actions driven by individuals within societies choosing to dissociate from organized religions. This is leading to far more enduring and profound changes – changes that are going to reshape human experience like never before.

It was heartening that, in the second half of 2020, both the Sudanese and Lebanese governments announced plans to secularize their legal systems. The Sudanese Justice Minister Nasreldin Abdelbari commented that the reforms would continue until his country had abolished "all the laws that violate human rights in Sudan", while the country's Prime Minister, Abdallah Hamdok, stated on his Twitter feed "I was pleased to speak today in a virtual meeting with human rights and civil society organisations from around the world, who remain strong allies of the Sudanese people in the path to change and democratisation. We look forward to regularly engaging with them and count on this continued partnership in realising the slogans of our revolution: Freedom, Peace and Justice."[13] The reforms included repealing a number of Islamic laws, such as those relating to apostasy, alcohol and female dress codes. The accord ends 30 years of rule under Islamic law and of Islam as the official state religion. The agreement declares that "the state shall not establish an official religion" and that "no citizen shall be discriminated against based on their religion".[14] The moves are inspired by the principle of separation of religion and state.

Lebanon has for decades been divided under sectarian rules that required the president to be a Maronite Christian, the Prime Minister to be a Sunni Muslim and the Speaker of the Parliament to be a Shi'a Muslim. The new President, Michel Aoun, announced in a speech to the nation in August that "Lebanon's youth are calling for change … for them and for their future" and that he recognized the need to "change the system". He backed this up by saying, "I call for the proclamation of Lebanon as a secular state." He also advised that this was the only way "of protecting and preserving pluralism".[15]

Having the governments of these two troubled countries acknowledge that a secular state is the best way forward could create a snowball effect in nearby Arab and Muslim nations. If members of these other nations observe improved peace and freedoms, more inclusive systems and an improved quality of life, then they may also demand similar changes from their governments in the next few years.

CHAPTER 4
THE WHEAT FROM THE CHAFF

Religions have been an integral component of our existence since we first developed the ability to contemplate cause and effect and began internalizing the fear of death. Believing that something outside us could be the source of our success or misery allowed people to share with each other a modicum of burden in difficult times. Religions subsequently gave rise to complex institutions and beliefs that made people feel more protected from misfortune and natural disasters.

Today, however, we have a greater understanding of catastrophes, disease and food shortages, and can take steps to mitigate them. The times of praying for rain, or propitiating a deity are fading rapidly; we can turn to scientific solutions rather than wishful thinking.

Nevertheless, there are still some aspects of religions that could continue to benefit people, during and beyond the inevitable shift to secular systems and ideologies. Let's take a look at some of them, their pros and cons, and possible alternatives.

Providing comfort

Pros: Religions have long offered explanations and interpretations of life that have provided comfort to those who require it. These explanations can help alleviate feelings of uncertainty and appease feelings of insecurity. They can provide useful coping mechanisms and stability when life seems unstable, thereby reducing stress. They reassure believers that a divine overlord will protect them and all will be well, engendering a feeling of being loved and valued in individuals even if those around them are not providing this, a feeling of being heard, important and understood. Faith, in a religious context, can be a positive force and help ease one's concerns; it can bring hope for something better in times of uncertainty, and be a practical tool as well as an emotional crutch. To allow oneself to be disencumbered and assuaged of certain fears can be extremely beneficial, especially when a group shares common beliefs.

Cons: Many religious explanations are being shown to have no basis and are often false. They utilize guilt as a tool to keep one attached to the belief system. Those who try to follow the rules but find it impossible to comply and feel judged all the time can suffer much mental anguish. Even those who wish for a divine overlord must feel like they are being let down by him or ignored or, worse, made to feel somehow at fault. Religious faith often allows people to ignore evidence, which can be to the detriment of both themselves and those around them; this "blind faith" can be fertile ground for many forms of abuse. As Nobel laureate Steven Weinberg once said: "With or without religion, you would have good people doing good things and evil people doing evil things. But for good people to do evil things, that takes religion." [16]

Alternatives: Embracing verifiable evidence is an authentic way to live one's life and diminishes the need to question the validity of one's views. Though possibly appearing less reassuring than religious doctrines, once fully embraced, the resulting perspectives can be more comforting to many.

Purpose to life

Pros: Religious adherents are taught to find meaning in repetitive practices that connect them to their deity and something far grander than life on earth. These teachings can provide a helpful set of values, structures and routines to follow, including guidelines on how one can contribute to one's community.

Cons: Repeatedly performing or being involved with religious rituals can "inoculate" people against thinking rationally. Many beliefs are misleading, falsely comforting and hide the truth. If a devotee begins to question the validity of any instilled teachings, it can create discomfort and internal conflict.

Alternatives: The reality of us all being irrelevant to the universe is disappointing to many and something that a lot of people do not wish to ponder.

The fact that the universe would function completely fine if we never exist-ed makes most religious people uncomfortable or brings them to a state of denial. Being insignificant to the universe, however, does not mean being insignificant to those around us. We are capable of having positive influences in many important spheres of our existence. We can easily make our lives rewarding in an abundance of ways and we can also, as individuals, make a difference to the entire planet. We can have rewarding relationships or raise a family, be involved in communal activities and help out others locally and globally. We can enrich our lives by creating music or art, entertain others through theatre, television, movies or sport, or just put a smile on someone else's face by telling a joke or giving them a hug. You can go for a walk, go out for a meal or spend time with family or friends. These are in fact the most meaningful things for most people.

Despite the efforts of religious leaders to show that life is meaningless without belief in their deity, non-belief can be more genuine and rewarding and of course offer greater freedoms: freedom of choice; freedom of roles for women; freedom of lifestyle; freedom from restrictions on attire, prohibitions on music and alcohol in Islam; freedom to love and share life with whomever you want.

Being part of a community

Pros: Religions make it easy for people to share a common framework, in-cluding laws, rites, festivities and foods. Collective prayer and having regular structured gatherings may forge a sense of togetherness. This can be a great benefit to those who feel isolated or lonely or in need of deeper connections. Just by attending religious gatherings people may feel accepted and necessary. Fellow congregants support each other and the gathering place – a church, mosque or other hall – can be a place of refuge and safety. Leaders and con-gregants encourage each other to the best versions of themselves.

Cons: Religions create an "us versus them" divide, encouraging followers to view other religions as false and their adherents as wrong about their beliefs. Within each religion, sects have been created as a result of smaller groups believing that the way they practice is right while criticizing the practices of others. On top of that, if a follower no longer accepts all of the tenets and rituals of his or her group, then they may have to leave and find another as-sembly and risk being ostracized from their original community.

Alternatives: Many religious festivities are changing and becoming secularized. For example, the way the majority of people celebrate Christmas – by having a Christmas tree with decorations, presents and family get-togethers – has no deity-based attachment. This trend is increasingly allowing people from any background to celebrate all-inclusive global festivities.

Beyond religious groups, there are of course many other communities we can belong to, beginning with local and national cultural associations and events. People around the world enjoy national holidays such as Thanksgiving, Memorial Day and Independence Day, as well as the originally Pagan festival of Halloween. Such secular celebrations are likely to become more relevant and enhanced if religious holidays have less significance.

Structured weekly gatherings

Pros: Many adherents enjoy the routine of attending services on particular days and see it as a chance to disconnect from the busyness of society and have a short period of "reset time".

Cons: With people being less interested in the routine of attending services on set days, and business and trading now open seven days a week, societal structures and needs have changed. Gone are the days of working Monday to Friday and then attending a religious service when there were few other options at the weekend. Religions continue to run on schedules that are often too structured for modern society. Surveys across the globe show that the younger generations especially are decreasingly interested in attending regular prayer services.

Alternatives: Regular human interaction can be enjoyed at other regular gatherings such as sports events, hobby groups and other non-religious clubs and societies. Furthermore, if one wants to connect with others to discuss shared interests it can now be done, as has been shown during the Covid-19 pandemic, online, at any time of the day or night, with people from all corners of the globe. And you can now listen to and watch recordings, and discuss issues from, a far wider range of sources.

Family rituals

Pros: Practising religious rituals, such as pre-meal prayers, and celebrating religious festivals at home can strengthen family relationships. Regularly attending a religious institution together can also help unite and re-centre everyone. Important annual festivities can bring scattered families back together for a time, and recalling such events can give family life greater meaning.

Cons: When members of a family do not hold the same beliefs, religious practices can create deep divisions, alienating and sometimes ostracizing those who do not conform to expectations.

Alternatives: As major annual religious festivities become progressively secularized, they can be utilized by non-believers in a similar way – to bring families together and have them share rich and rewarding experiences. However, secularism faces challenges in bringing family members together on a more regular basis, as it currently lacks similarly binding daily or weekly rituals. Having a family "pizza night" does not compare to the formalized practices that religions have developed over the centuries. Attending sports or cultural events can be uniting, for example, but it doesn't perhaps attain the same sense of belonging or togetherness.

Further enhancements need to occur here. We must figure out how to create deeper and more bonding periodic familial practices. One such option could be to embrace coming-of-age celebrations. For example, greater emphasis could be placed on the ages when voting and/or driving are allowed in each community. These are major milestones in one's life and signify acceptance into the adult community and an acknowledgement of the related responsibility that comes with such privileges.

Wouldn't it be fantastic if governments also helped mark such events by strongly encouraging and rewarding voter registration? Young adults could also be taught to give back to the community through days of volunteering, donating blood, and so on. Perhaps each young person would be urged to participate in at least five communal good deeds each year. Secular societies certainly have the potential to create society-wide, positive and meaningful rituals.

Communal values

Pros: Religions foster the concept of communal values and the common good instead of self-interest, which is essential for creating a more altruistic society. Repeatedly being reminded of good values has the potential to create generosity of spirit and actions.

Cons: Problems can result when commitment to an organization is absolute or near absolute. The child abuse that has come to light in the last two decades was allowed to occur because the reputation of the relevant institution was seen as more important than the rights of individuals.

Alternatives: Closer monitoring of religious groups and greater willingness to call out poor behaviour and praise good acts in the media are changing this situation. Videos are often rapidly shared on social media of people performing good or bad deeds. The reality is that in most developed countries we have established secular legal systems and highly interactive communities to deal with poor behaviour. We no longer require the fear of a deity to coerce people to behave appropriately.

Being a source of moral values

Pros: Having texts that discuss acceptable and non-acceptable behaviours can create a shared moral framework, which is then regularly reinforced if people are regular attendees of services.

Cons: Many behaviours that are deemed immoral are either ridiculous (god will be offended if you eat pork or work on the Sabbath, for example) or unfair to or prejudiced against large sections of the community (homosexuality is a sin, women are of lesser value). Despite secularism knocking down the door on these values from the outside, many of these detestable pronouncements are still part of religious teachings.

Alternatives: Thankfully, most people worldwide are bound by secular legal codes, not religious ones, and religious pronouncements carry increasingly less weight.. Secular codes allow for changes over time, which have in turn made for more reasonable and just societies. If not for the expansion of secularist thought, slavery would still be seen as acceptable and women would not have access to the same opportunities as men.

Charity

Pros: Religions doctrines often encourage charitable behaviour, and for centuries churches and other religious organizations were the main source of support for people in times of difficulty. Many religious charities have done an enormous amount to feed and clothe those in need. Think of The Salvation Army, the Red Cross, World Vision and so on.

Cons: There are nearly always strings attached when religious organizations provide support, especially in developing nations. Missionaries are not going to these places purely out of the goodness of their hearts. Although their actions appear altruistic, as well as trying to convert the indigenous population they are undoubtedly also hoping that they will be rewarded for such acts by their god. Jomo Kenyatta, the first President of Kenya, is said to have observed, "When the missionaries arrived the Africans had the land and the missionaries had the Bible. They taught us how to pray with our eyes closed. When we opened them, they had the land and we had the Bible."

Alternatives: Organized religions have for centuries dominated charities and relief works, but this is changing. The United Nations, which came into existence in 1945, has established numerous secular, global support bodies, including:

- **UNFPA** – United Nations Population Fund
- **UNICEF** – United Nations Children's Fund
- **WFP** – World Food Programme
- **FAO** – Food and Agriculture Organization
- **IFAD** – International Fund for Agricultural Development
- **UNIDO** – United Nations Industrial Development Organization

On top of this, there are now thousands of secular charities that exist across the globe, including Amnesty International, Relief International, OXFAM, WaterAid, Médecins Sans Frontières (Doctors Without Borders) and KIVA, an interesting charity that receives and distributes donations solely online. In every country there are a myriad of non-religious support groups that people can belong to or donate to, especially in times of crisis, and many charitable foundations have been created by multinational companies, wealthy families and trusts.

I have no doubt that religious "corporations" are fighting hard in the background to continue to be viewed as the leading suppliers of charitable services. They will battle to protect these arms of their business models, otherwise they run the risk of losing their tax-exempt status, which currently extends to every facet of their activities, including commercial ventures.

Religious leaders

Pros: Traditionally, clergy are admired and respected figureheads, who lead followers in religious services and rituals. They are also usually trusted individuals whom people can approach for life advice. They may have spent most of their adult lives helping people deal with moral issues and crises and have interesting philosophical viewpoints which it can be advantageous to share. They are often supportive, non-judgmental and forgiving, so that people feel safe disclosing things to them. On top of this, their advice is normally free and unlimited!

Cons: The reality is that although religious leaders are educated, their viewpoints are often narrow and constrained by their dogma. They may have little real experience of life – for example, never having had sexual relationships or been married – which means they may not fully understand its complexities. Also, having to adhere to the strict rules of their religion can make dealing with crises much more difficult. In some cases the only advice they can offer on an issue like abortion or divorce is not to do it, under any circumstances.

Alternatives: Secular institutions are creating an infinitely greater knowledge base that is accessible to everyone and producing specialists in life advice who are able to provide much broader, less constrained and biased guidance. Trained psychologists, for example, have deeper and more relevant experience and can provide far more effective tools for dealing with traumas and crises. Unfortunately, this knowledge is not usually free!

And when it comes to presiding over rituals, religious figures are not always required. Many more people are already availing themselves of the services of civil celebrants for weddings, for example, and enjoying the freedom that such options bring.

Spirituality

Spirituality is a worldview that holds that there is more to life than just what people experience on a physical or sensory level; it is a belief in something beyond the self. Though religion and spirituality are not interchangeable terms, religions have long claimed ownership of the concept of spirituality.

Pros: Religions have created foundational structures and teachings that seek to show that there is something awe-inspiring and greater than us that will allow us to live eternally. This form of spirituality creates a powerful feeling of being in touch with something that science cannot see and a sense that we can connect more deeply with our departed loved ones, with each other, with ourselves and with the wider universe. Believing that there is a positive energy source that is available for us to tap into or transfer to after death can be comforting and reassuring.

Cons: Focusing on a form of spirituality derived from only one religion's texts narrows one's spiritual outlook and potential resources.

Alternatives: Since the middle of the last century there has been an upswing in interest among Westerners in some Buddhist and Hindu practices. It is not unusual for Jews and Christians, for example, to dabble in meditation and yoga, which are perceived as bringing general health benefits. People can now seek inner peace and spirituality through a much wider array of practices than are available through a single religious experience.

One of the advantages of non-theistic spirituality over the dogma of organized religions is that it can be a far more immediate, intimate and personal experience. Religions are usually based on events in history, whereas a more varied and wide-ranging form of spirituality can seem timeless and not constrained by structured calendars. One can choose to engage in spiritually enhancing practices at any time of the day or night, or any day of the year.

We need to enhance access to a wide range of religious thought and philosophies and adapt them for our secular world, so that they can be tapped into by anyone, anywhere, at any time – even by groups utilizing technology to facilitate co-ordinated spiritual interactions with family and friends. For example, people have already begun to hold online yoga and meditation classes, and a huge range of lectures and podcasts on spiritual topics, from across the globe, is available on demand.

A source of knowledge

Pros: For a long time, the stories that religions told about God, the soul and life after death provided an explanation of the origins of our world and a comforting narrative that set out why we are here and what we must do.

Cons: Religious teachings and beliefs have often been obstacles to scientific progress. For most of their history, religions have claimed their fables to be truisms, whereas we can now see that they are undoubtedly human creations. As science increasingly proves religious truths to be falsehoods, religions are forced to qualify their claims, often moving the goalposts to assert that "science explains the how but religion the why".

Alternatives: Science has achieved many remarkable advances in recent times, some of which have been vehemently opposed by religions with false, patently false claims such as:

Condoms: "Sexually transmitted diseases are a message from God."
Euthanasia: "Only God can decide when a human being can die."
IVF: "Only God can create human beings."
Stem cell research: "Only God can make these decisions."

In general, any scientific knowledge that goes against the ancient texts is initially denied, then argued against; but once the evidence is overwhelming, religions tend to change their view and claim that rather than being literally true their stories are important "metaphors".

Deity religions also teach dominion over nature, whereas an evolutionary understanding creates greater respect for all living things. As has been seen, religious literalists tend to be less concerned about human damage to the environment than the non-religious. The world might be better off if we revived some early animist beliefs and showed more respect for other creatures as well as the environment.

We should no longer be turning to religions as sources of "knowledge", but we can still draw on religious teachings and stories to develop more progressive spiritual philosophies.

Wisdom

Pros: Religions have gathered thousands of years of deep thinking to create fantastic theological and philosophical resources. There is an enormous amount of wisdom in the sacred texts that we can draw on to help us deal with the many challenges of human existence.

Cons: It should be evident that while all religions contain some wisdom, no one religion contains all wisdom. Why then limit ourselves? There is so much wisdom, insight and deep thought out there. If people are raised within a single religion, they miss out on so many opportunities to learn and further themselves.

Alternatives: We should not have to be frugal with wisdom; we should be encouraging it to come into our lives from as many sources as possible. Only then can we maximize our potential. As a small exercise in showing this, the following is a sample of quotes from the Chinese philosopher Confucius, which most people are not exposed to on a regular basis but which can inspire thoughtful and remarkably advantageous mindsets:

"The man who moves a mountain begins by carrying away small stones."

"If you make a mistake and do not correct it, this is called a mistake."

"Study the past if you would define the future."

"Before you embark on a journey of revenge, dig two graves."

"The man who asks a question is a fool for a minute; the man who does not ask is a fool for life."

"The gem cannot be polished without friction, nor man perfected without trials."

"The man who says he can and the man who says he cannot are both correct."

"We have two lives, and the second begins when we realize we only have one."

"If your plan is for one year, plant rice. If your plan is for ten years, plant trees. If your plan is for one hundred years, educate children."

"It is easy to hate and difficult to love. This is how the whole scheme of things works. All good things are difficult to achieve, and bad things are very easy to obtain."

"The superior man is modest in his speech but exceeds in his actions."

Imagine a world where people were regularly exposed to wisdom from all of the world's religions and philosophies.

Inspiration

Pros The sense among religious people that they have a connection with the being that created everything can truly engender a sense of awe. And awe is an amazing emotion that should inspire us to act for higher purposes, chase the pleasures of life and regularly stop and smell the roses. Some of the world's greatest works of architecture, art and music were inspired by religions. One only has to look at some of the amazing churches throughout Europe, the mosques in the Muslim World, or Hindu and Buddhist temples in Asia to appreciate what humankind is capable of creating when inspired by religious awe and wonder.

Cons: Relying on religion severely limits our potential sources of awe and wonder by tying us to narrow belief systems and obstructing scientific wonderment. We should be moving on from the belief in a deity who ignores or treats the majority of humankind with disdain and contempt.

Alternatives: While religious feeling is one potential source of awe, there are many others available to us. Our natural yearning for a sense of wonder can be satiated by standing in front of a majestic waterfall or walking along a beautiful beach. Watching children running barefoot on the sand and seeing the delight in their faces as they play in the shallows and jump over waves brings a sense of joy and exhilaration that is often missing from religious experiences.

The setting sun can be one of the most magical and magnificent sights to behold as it lights up the sky as if it were on fire then slowly dims and disappears below the horizon. Music can elevate us to happy places and bring back pleasurable memories. There is no need for a deity in order to have a life filled with wonder and joy.

Non-theists can also experience wonderment without the shackles of religious teachings by learning to appreciate the scientific principles behind innumerable, amazing natural phenomena. And they can be further inspired by the thought that many of the mysteries of life will eventually be solved by science. This is far more exciting than the dead end of "God did it", and is what drives many researchers in their search for answers.

Conclusions

Nearly everything that religions offer can be provided just as satisfactorily, if not more so, by secular institutions and ideologies and natural phenomena. While there are still some areas of shortfall, these can undoubtedly be focused on in the coming years to ensure that the offerings to humanity are improved on what we have today.

CHAPTER 5
PRIORITIES MOVING FORWARDS

We are on the cusp of a brand-new internet-connected era, when potentially each person on the planet can interact with everyone else – an astonishing concept considering there are now approaching eight billion humans on earth. For the first time ever, we are a globally connected species. This gives us the potential to decide on future common systems for all of humankind, and, without a doubt, this means that the constraints of geography and religious indoctrination will soon become irrelevant.

Going forwards, we can create more unified, unifying and universal belief systems, frameworks of concepts that people can opt into or out of on a needs basis. These codes would be based on evolving morality, laws and guidelines and would be entirely inclusive, ultimately providing equal rights for all. Such philosophies would provide much broader and more varied ways to nourish the mind and "soul" (I'm using the term metaphorically) than anything a single religion can offer.

As a starting point, we must recognize that all humans:
- are born incomplete and depend on others within their community to survive and thrive
- must form social relationships to exist and flourish
- must learn to deal with the many challenges that confront us in life, including sickness, suffering and death
- reside in a world where forces exist that are bigger and more powerful than them – natural, social, economic and political.

Instead of abiding by ancient dogmatic religious rules, our new humanistic philosophical structures should draw on the great documents drawn up
by the world's most progressive societies – such as the English Bill of Rights,
US Bill of Rights, the French Declaration of the Rights of Man and of the
Citizen, and the United Nations Universal Declaration of Human Rights –
as the starting point for a global framework. I am confident that by the end of
this century a formalized conglomeration of these concepts will have become
the dominant societal code of the world, and that by then religious stricture
and structure will have faded into the background.

An interesting framework was created at the 50th anniversary World
Humanist Congress, held in the Netherlands in the year 2002. At the event,
the body's general assembly passed a resolution known as "The Amsterdam
Declaration 2002"; its official defining statement was:

- Humanism is ethical. It affirms the worth, dignity and autonomy of the
  individual and the right of every human being to the greatest possible
  freedom compatible with the rights of others. Humanists have a duty of
  care to all humanity including future generations. Humanists believe that
  morality is an intrinsic part of human nature based on understanding and
  a concern for others, needing no external sanction.
- Humanism is rational. It seeks to use science creatively, not destructive-
  ly. Humanists believe that the solutions to the world's problems lie in
  human thought and action rather than divine intervention. Humanism
  advocates the application of the methods of science and free inquiry to
  the problems of human welfare. But Humanists also believe that the application of science and technology must be tempered by human values.
  Science gives us the means, but human values must propose the ends.
- Humanism supports democracy and human rights. Humanism aims at
  the fullest possible development of every human being. It holds that democracy and human development are matters of right. The principles of
  democracy and human rights can be applied to many human relationships and are not restricted to methods of government.
- Humanism insists that personal liberty must be combined with social
  responsibility. Humanism ventures to build a world on the idea of the
  free person responsible to society, and recognizes our dependence and
  responsibility for the natural world. Humanism is undogmatic, imposing
  no creed upon its adherents. It is thus committed to education free from
  indoctrination.

- Humanism is a response to the widespread demand for an alternative to dogmatic religion. The world's major religions claim to be based on revelations fixed for all time, and many seek to impose their worldview on all of humanity. Humanism recognizes that reliable knowledge of the world and ourselves arises through a continuing process of observation, evaluation and revision.

- Humanism values artistic creativity and imagination and recognizes the transforming power of art. Humanism affirms the importance of literature, music, and the visual and performing arts for personal development and fulfilment.

- Humanism is a life-stance aiming at the maximum possible fulfilment through the cultivation of ethical and creative living and offers an ethical and rational means of addressing the challenges of our time. Humanism can be a way of life for everyone everywhere.[17]

Most importantly, The Amsterdam Declaration explicitly states that Humanism rejects dogma and imposes no creed upon its adherents. Although I am not fond of the term "Humanism", as it implies that humans are the paramount creatures on the planet, the declaration itself is a far better societal foundation than the Ten Commandments (the first three of which relate to appeasing the God of the Old Testament and the fourth to resting on the Sabbath).

World wars have been fought, with millions killed, yet only a short number of years pass and civilians from opposing nations start to get along fine. Wars in the name of religion, on the other hand, have resulted in millions of deaths over thousands of years, and there is no end in sight to these divisions and conflicts. In many cases, religious leaders foment and exploit these divisions to maintain sovereignty over their adherents and they act in ways only possible if one feels as though they are following the orders of a higher authority (bemoaned in secular circles as The Nuremberg Defence). These attitudes must be eradicated from our civilizations if we are to create a better world for everyone.

The Covid-19 pandemic has in fact shown for the first time how interconnected people are across the globe. There is widespread sharing of information and policy strategies in an effort to contain and eventually treat this now-ubiquitous virus. Scientists, politicians, policy makers and healthcare professionals have been working collaboratively, in many cases for the first time in order to eradicate the disease. As an atheist, I can happily draw a parallel with what is happening, albeit at a much slower rate, with regards to religions! If we can construct common goals in the arena of disease eradication, then perhaps soon we can begin transitioning towards a respectful humanist societal framework encompassing all citizens of the world.

It is evident that we are yet to create apex societies. We have come a long way in the last century; life is currently the safest it has ever been during humankind's existence, with homelessness, disease and starvation being at their lowest levels. Life expectancy has continued to increase while working hours have been reduced. We have more leisure time than ever before to enjoy the fruits of our labours. With the proliferation of artificial intelligence (AI) and mechanized systems, the hours we spend working are likely to be further reduced.

So let's take it upon ourselves over the next few decades to create systems that allow anyone to belong and that focus on constructive, positive and inclusive guidance principles.

Making our own judgments

With AI and high-definition cameras expected to be almost everywhere in the next few decades, it will be virtually impossible to commit a crime without it being recorded. Though this idea conjures up negative Orwellian connotations of "Big Brother", the technology will help us move beyond the need for "the man in the clouds" (just as, ironically, increasing amounts of our data, and our lives, are being stored there).

We no longer need to refer back to religious texts to look for solutions to moral dilemmas. Modern philosophy and healthy debate have shown themselves far more capable of dealing with current issues than the ancient texts. If we were following their judgments, we would still believe that a crime should be paid for on the basis of "an eye for an eye", that women are of lesser value and that slavery is acceptable.

New laws will soon have to be introduced to regulate autonomous vehicles, so where will lawmakers look? I have no doubt that they will be calling on professors of philosophy rather than priests, rabbis and imams. Religious leaders are no longer required in contemporary society for moral or legal guidance: their views are too narrow and constrained by their own textual doctrines. Although religious leaders were previously viewed as intermediaries between the common folk and their deity and as saintly moral authorities on whom humanity could depend for guidance, what has become clear in recent years, as a result of widespread investigations and publicity, is that they are all too human, engaging in sinful behaviours both as individuals and institutions. This has greatly diminished their standing and people's respect for them.

The keys to happiness

If religions are receding, how does that allow us to improve our societies? What should our objectives be?

Life satisfaction and happiness are two of the most important areas to focus on to improve our lives. Though they sound similar, these concepts are actually quite distinct. Happiness is a fleeting experience, while life satisfaction is a long-term feeling based on achieving goals and building the kind of existence that you desire.

In 1972, the fourth King of Bhutan, Jigme Singye Wangchuck, coined the phrase Gross National Happiness, or GNH, in an attempt to redefine how we assess the most important aspects of human success. While economic statistics are important indicators of a society's development, the king pointed out, other, non-economic data must be considered when attempting to determine whether a society is achieving improving the happiness and well-being of its members. In 2011 the UN General Assembly, following up on King Wangchuck's suggestion, adopted a resolution to invite member countries to measure the happiness of their people, in order to help guide public policy. The six key measures were: income, social support, healthy life expectancy, freedom, generosity and perceptions of corruption. In 2012 the United Nations released its first annual report outlining the state of world happiness, the causes of happiness and misery, and the policy implications of these findings. It asked for GNH to become the main developmental indicator for countries instead of GDP.

Analyses of GNH have shown clearly that countries with the highest percentage of non-believers are amongst the most considerate, happy societies, and have the highest life expectancies. The following tables are from the 2019 "World Happiness Report". The top countries on the list are nearly all among the most secular nations on the planet.

Overall rank	Country or region	Score	GDP per capita	Social support	Healthy life expectancy	Freedom to make life choices	Generosity	Perceptio of corruptic
1	Finland	7.769	1.340	1.587	0.986	0.596	0.153	0.393
2	Denmark	7.600	1.383	1.573	0.996	0.592	0.252	0.410
3	Norway	7.554	1.488	1.582	1.028	0.603	0.271	0.341
4	Iceland	7.494	1.380	1.624	1.026	0.591	0.354	0.118
5	Netherlands	7.488	1.396	1.522	0.999	0.557	0.322	0.298
6	Switzerland	7.480	1.452	1.526	1.052	0.572	0.263	0.343
7	Sweden	7.343	1.387	1.487	1.009	0.574	0.267	0.373
8	New Zealand	7.307	1.303	1.557	1.026	0.585	0.330	0.380
9	Canada	7.278	1.365	1.505	1.039	0.584	0.285	0.308
10	Austria	7.246	1.376	1.475	1.016	0.532	0.244	0.226
11	Australia	7.228	1.372	1.548	1.036	0.557	0.332	0.290
12	Costa Rica	7.167	1.034	1.441	0.963	0.558	0.144	0.093
13	Israel	7.139	1.276	1.455	1.029	0.371	0.261	0.082
14	Luxembourg	7.090	1.609	1.479	1.012	0.526	0.194	0.316
15	United Kingdom	7.054	1.333	1.538	0.996	0.450	0.348	0.278

Image 52

Conversely, the bottom countries in the table are among the most religious societies. Other studies confirm that the most religious nations often have the highest levels of poverty, income inequality between the sexes and restrictions on personal freedom.

134	Ethiopia	4.286	0.336	1.033	0.532	0.344	0.209	0.100
135	Eswatini	4.212	0.811	1.149	0.000	0.313	0.074	0.135
136	Uganda	4.189	0.332	1.069	0.443	0.356	0.252	0.060
137	Egypt	4.166	0.913	1.039	0.644	0.241	0.076	0.067
138	Zambia	4.107	0.578	1.058	0.426	0.431	0.247	0.087
139	Togo	4.085	0.275	0.572	0.410	0.293	0.177	0.085
140	India	4.015	0.755	0.765	0.588	0.498	0.200	0.085
141	Liberia	3.975	0.073	0.922	0.443	0.370	0.233	0.033
142	Comoros	3.973	0.274	0.757	0.505	0.142	0.275	0.078
143	Madagascar	3.933	0.274	0.916	0.555	0.148	0.169	0.041
144	Lesotho	3.802	0.489	1.169	0.168	0.359	0.107	0.093
145	Burundi	3.775	0.046	0.447	0.380	0.220	0.176	0.180
146	Zimbabwe	3.663	0.366	1.114	0.433	0.361	0.151	0.089
147	Haiti	3.597	0.323	0.688	0.449	0.026	0.419	0.110
148	Botswana	3.488	1.041	1.145	0.538	0.455	0.025	0.100
149	Syria	3.462	0.619	0.378	0.440	0.013	0.331	0.141
150	Malawi	3.410	0.191	0.560	0.495	0.443	0.218	0.089
151	Yemen	3.380	0.287	1.163	0.463	0.143	0.108	0.077
152	Rwanda	3.334	0.359	0.711	0.614	0.555	0.217	0.411
153	Tanzania	3.231	0.476	0.885	0.499	0.417	0.276	0.147
154	Afghanistan	3.203	0.350	0.517	0.361	0.000	0.158	0.025
155	Central African Republic	3.083	0.026	0.000	0.105	0.225	0.235	0.035
156	South Sudan	2.853	0.306	0.575	0.295	0.010	0.202	0.091

Image 53

This does not necessarily imply causation – that reduced religiosity leads to a more content society – and many would argue that belonging to a more stable, open and economically advanced society simply allows for a reduced dependence on religion.

More specifically, studies have shown that people who reside in a society where the government provides a broader and stronger welfare system are less reliant on religion. In other words, when people feel supported by their governments, communities or fellow human beings, they are less likely to depend on a supernatural deity to look after them.

As Karl Marx once wrote, "Religious suffering is, at one and the same time, the expression of real suffering and a protest against real suffering. Religion is the sigh of the oppressed creature, the heart of a heartless world, and the soul of soulless conditions. It is the opium of the people."[18] What he was alluding to is that if the society that one lives in does not support you, then religions may fill the void.

This may help explain why the United States has a more steadfast religious culture than all other highly developed nations, as its welfare system is much less supportive than those of the countries higher up the "World Happiness" list (the United States sits at number 18 in the above table). Socialist ideals are still seen as anathema by many Americans, who consider them a threat to their way of life, despite the evidence that they often lead to better societies.

So, why are some societies more successful than others at achieving both individual and collective well-being? How should societies be amended to improve these essential metrics? We are by and large social creatures, so how do we improve patterns of social relations by building better institutional and cultural practices?

Based on the UN findings, some of the characteristics of a happy society are that it
• provides stable employment
• ensures a safe environment
• provides free or subsidized healthcare
• offers ample access for all members of a society to free or subsidized good-quality education
• ensures that there are reasonable back-up systems during times of trouble
• cultivates kindness
• encourages tolerance

- allows its citizens to freely question government
- fosters ingenuity and hope
- offers women full equality and freedoms, including equal access to education, jobs and other opportunities (this is particularly pertinent vis-à-vis religious countries).

All governments should allocate significant funds to achieving these goals, as it has been clearly shown that this will result in profound improvements in the lives of citizens and reduce the relevance and importance of religions.

Challenges facing secularism

Religions have had over two thousand years to create doctrines, rules and institutions, many of which are still deeply embedded in societies and the lives of families and individuals. Secularism as a movement has thus far not succeeded in comprehensively penetrating the minds of the masses; in part, this is because it has rejected and distanced itself from anything associated with religious organizations. Yet, we need not discard all of the concepts and structures of religions because many are still valuable and relevant to many people.

It would be sensible if over the next few decades, secularism drew ideas and inspiration from the constructs of *all* faiths; that way, it might garner greater support from a much wider range of people from disparate backgrounds. After all, Christianity did this in its first few centuries and it has become the most widespread belief system of the planet!

A deficiency of the secular world is that it is constantly bringing in new ideas and looks down on old practices. Secular knowledge is easily ignored and forgotten as we move on to the next sound bite without regularly and repetitively re-engaging with useful concepts. This is a major shortcoming, as human beings derive much comfort from repetition and are unsettled by always being presented with new information and changing procedures. The obsession with new ideas undermines the reassuring sense of permanence that religions provide.

Religions have successfully established structured calendars and routines to define precisely what adherents must read; the daily, even hourly, rules and rituals they must follow; when and how to think (or not); and when to gather to celebrate aspects of their beliefs. To be successful, secular systems need to adopt, or adapt, some of these practices, for example by initiating regular national or international celebrations or gatherings involving meaningful, repeated rituals, so that people become comfortable and familiar with the ideals of secularism and feel more connected to its cause.

Aside from the many national days that countries around the world celebrate, there are no regular national or international secular celebrations or festivals that compare in scale and depth with religious ones. It would be difficult to initiate them from scratch, so it seems reasonable and entirely sensible to instead adopt the framework of some pre-existing holidays and secularize them further. For example, I would love to see people worldwide celebrate aspects of the traditional South Asian festival of Diwali in a secularized form. The overarching concept of the "victory of light over darkness, good over evil and knowledge over ignorance" is celebrated by lighting one's house with candles and lanterns, dressing in fine clothes, and holding family feasts with traditional foods. It would also be of benefit to participate in a modified form of the Jewish Day of Atonement or Ramadan, whereby a day-long fast is undertaken to remind us to re-centre ourselves and donate time and/or money to less fortunate people.

As discussed in my previous book, we could also look at promoting and adapting some of the recognized but little known "World Days". These include:

March 3	World Wildlife Day
March 20	International Day of Happiness
April 7	World Health Day
May 15	International Day of Families
June 5	World Environment Day
September 5	International Day of Charity
October 1	International Day of Older Persons
December 31	New Year's Eve

To make these days more meaningful, we would need to develop associated rituals and customs that would make people feel more involved and help them understand the day's significance. Undoubtedly, our social systems can be greatly enhanced to create inclusive festivities that would be more relevant, appropriate, engaging and gratifying than current secular celebrations.

The poetic mind

Religious texts have heroes and underdog stories that, when retold over and over, make us feel that maybe we too can overcome the next challenge that life will throw at us and that suffering will give way to joy and success. The most vital point in the story of Jesus, for example, is how he was treated poorly and suffered to the end yet ended up residing eternally alongside God.

The religious promise of a trouble-free eternal existence after an often arduous earthly life is a pleasing narrative for many people. The fact that the secular world cannot offer such reassurance (or, as atheists see it, a comforting lie versus a painful truth) is for many people a distinct disadvantage.

Moreover, the sacred texts of Muslims, Christians and Jews were written and closed off over 1500 years ago and have been quoted and requoted to followers since then, making their core teachings easy to remember and follow. There are arguably as many great lessons in secular writings – imagine if we could all be informed and motivated by the works of Homer, Aesop, Aristotle, Lao Tzu, Confucius, Buddha and Shakespeare – but without periodic re-engagement with such texts, we are unlikely to remember their wisdom in the way that people absorb religious teachings. Secular education "suffers" from an excess of material, and that can mean that the meaningful messages of important works are watered down. One person's favourite concepts from Tolstoy will not match another person's engagement with Mark Twain. With so many works to choose from, where does one turn to for sage advice? How much simpler to walk into a library of only a handful of religious texts?

People enjoy storytelling and the way its tales and metaphors can arouse and motivate the heart and mind. But in a world where young people are overwhelmed by a daily barrage of new narratives, it may be more profitable for secularism to direct their focus to stories of recent, real-life figures who have endured hardships, stood up against oppression or suffered or died for a cause – the likes of Nelson Mandela, for example, who campaigned for decades against the South African apartheid system and eventually rose to the position of President of South Africa.

Image 54

This kind of learning can begin in the school system, so that the interest in role models becomes an ingrained part of our ethos. Identifying heroes in a modern context is one of the driving forces behind social media and people regularly participate in discussions about such issues. We can still utilize stories and quotes from all of the religious texts, but we should "re-fictionalize" the characters, allowing society to utilize a much wider variety of profitable sources.

Although news and popular culture often have only fleeting significance, occasionally they spotlight people whose ideals we can connect with and/or use as inspirational or creative tools. For example, in June 1989 the Chinese Government sent in its army to crack down on a major protest against government corruption, lack of transparency and freedom of speech. In what has become known as the Tiananmen Square massacre, troops armed with assault rifles and accompanied by tanks killed hundreds of protestors occupying parts of central Beijing. As a column of tanks was departing the area, a lone man stood defiantly in its way and moved to block the tanks as they tried to move around him.[19] His actions were brave and motivating for people seeking freedom from tyranny worldwide.

Image 55

Sometimes the media do a good job of drawing attention to inspiring public figures. *Time* magazine, for instance, has an annual issue that identifies people who are making a difference in the world. We need to be able to connect with and focus on these inspirational people more, but unfortunately most current affairs media prefer to engage with negative stories than spend time exploring and spotlight uplifting and encouraging ones.

Is a replacement for religions required?

When I first started to consider this question, I based my conclusions on the thoughts of a middle-aged person who, like most people of my generation and older generations, had grown up in a community and society where religion was seen as indispensable and broadly respected. Many people of my age and older feel we have to pander to an innate human predisposition to believe in a creator and a higher order of things. This has in turn led us to accept the need for a more structured and ritualized community.

Yet young people today are like no previous generations. We might like to believe that our lives are far removed from those of our grandparents and those preceding them, but the gulf is far deeper and more pronounced for Millennials. They are the first generation to have been raised connected to the internet and absorbed in social media. Their upbringing has been like no other in the history of humankind.

I am firmly of the opinion that, for the first time in 100,000 years, there is a gulf between the developmental influence of internet-based interactions on this current generation and the nurturing received by any previous generation in history. The brains of our young people will be moulded in a way that no previous humans have experienced.

Up until now, we were raised in fairly small communities and the information we received and used to form our opinions came mainly from close contacts. But young people today are connected to others everywhere, source most of their information from the World-Wide Web and are influenced as much by social media as by their families and close community. Many of them spend much of their time interacting with groups of likeminded people on Facebook, Instagram and other social media platforms and participating in online gaming. They are strongly associated with an extremely broad base of people existing in the ether.

As a result, they may no longer require bricks-and-mortar institutions or even a cohesive pastoral community to guide them. Particularly if they already have strong familial connections, school groups, hobbies, sporting affiliations and a number of close friends, they may have no need for yet another social grouping such as a religion.

Young people today have global connections, live far more in the here and now, and are far less in need of mythology or religious texts to explain the world, especially when they have access to Google (and this is of course why so many fundamentalist religious groups deny their followers access to the online world). They are naturally sceptical of many of the historical claims made by religions.

As an example, witness their experience of the "marriage equality" debate. It was evident to them that secular society was bringing important rights to a significant minority group, and they saw that many religious institutions spent millions of dollars to fight tooth and nail against this move because it contradicted their dogma. And now that the dust has settled, only religious zealots speak out against homosexuality and gay marriage, and even religious moderates have been embarrassed into having to favour secular values over their religious doctrine.

As our planet's population approaches 8 billion people (a five-fold increase in just over a century), we are constantly being bombarded by information, influences, advertisements and promotions. Our lives are saturated by media and stories of other people, and many of us are constantly surrounded by other people, on public transport, at airports and on planes, in traffic, in office buildings, in shopping centres, at supermarkets and gym classes. Everywhere we turn, there are people!

Many of us are happy to take a break from the additional physical interaction with others that religion involves. We are content to close our front doors and have some respite from communal interactions. Though this has created feelings of isolation and loneliness for some, for many people technology and social media give them convenient control over their lives and the power to participate in society on their own terms and at their own pace, without the stress of being judged on their appearance – and in the comfort of a daggy old tracksuit or pyjamas!

What will replace religions?

Surveys have shown an ever-growing percentage of the population who see themselves a "spiritual but not religious". These people want to maintain some of the basic structures and ideologies of religions but without the theistic overtures or dogma. So will we start to see the emergence and development of broader spiritual communities in the real and online worlds?

Sunday Assembly, an organization set up to promote non-deity-based community gatherings, was founded in the United Kingdom in 2013. It has attempted to create a secular replacement for weekend religious services in the form of meetings where attendees listen to speakers, sing and discuss ethics and spiritual issues. But although there are now chapters of Sunday Assembly in a number of countries, it has not garnered significant popularity. Merely having a common non-belief does not appear to be enough to attract attendees on a regular basis. Meeting on a regular basis without a doctrine, without a historical perspective, without the fables and legends, and without the long-standing connections makes for a difficult build. That's not surprising really, given that it's becoming exceedingly difficult to get people to attend mass, even with all the power the Catholic Church wields and the guilt it engenders, and the chances of sustained success with this secular model seem low.

CHAPTER 6
WHERE TO NEXT?

How do we intentionally create successful societies while encouraging future generations to function effectively without religion? Religions were important when groups were more tribal and insular, but we now have a more homogenized world. Not only do we interact with people of all different backgrounds as never before, but "mixed" sexual relationships, de facto relationships and "intermarriage" are occurring at an ever-increasing rate. As a result, religious tribalisms are steadily becoming less and less relevant and influential.

Yet we can do more to ensure that the influence of religion continues to decline, and that our societies develop in an open, healthy way that benefits all its members equally. Effective secularization of society entails at least three different aspects:

1. Elimination of theological and deity-based thought from childhood education and government decision-making.
2. The removal of religious leaders and influences from positions of economic or political control.
3. Withdrawing the privileged roles religious institutions play in education, marriage and divorce, so that "the family" is legitimized by the state rather than the local religion.

Decision-making

Despite supposed separation of church and state, there are many entanglements of the two parties that should be removed, as they can be obstacles to creating impartial systems. Governments should treat everyone equally and not grant exemptions based on religious groupings. It is inequitable to create exceptions to the rule of law simply because a religion has long-standing beliefs or cultural or ritualistic practices. Many of these practices, such as Islamic and Jewish divorce laws, result in women being treated abominably, and there is no reason why we should continue to accept such legal "anomalies". Other damaging and objectionable religious traditions include infant or child circumcision, female genital mutilation, enforced dress codes for women, and allowing parents to make detrimental medical decisions on behalf of children simply because it is a part of their religious beliefs.

While parents must be allowed to make healthcare choices on behalf of their children, the state should have sufficient legal powers to ensure that religious beliefs do not endanger the well-being of a child. Adults are entitled to make personally detrimental decisions about their own welfare, but not to reject a treatment for a child on religious grounds if it will, say, save the child's life.

To further disentangle church from state, societies should prevent practices such as:

- religious movements participating in political systems
- opening and closing parliamentary sessions with prayers
- depicting or referring to deities on national currencies
- referring to deities in national anthems (for example, "God save the Queen")
- swearing on the Bible in a courtroom
- allowing religious leaders to influence medical and other welfare services
- granting blanket tax-exempt status to religions.

Economic development

Economic development of a society is often closely related to education levels and both often show an inverse relationship to religious adherence. As poverty levels decrease and education and other social services improve in a country, concern about day-to-day survival diminishes, in turn reducing the need for the emotional crutch that religion can provide. Therefore, if the world continues to raise living standards and lift more people out of poverty, we will likely observe a steady decline in loyalty to religions.

Share of population living in extreme poverty by world region

Extreme poverty is defined as living with less than 1.90$ per day (in 2011 International Dollar). International dollars are adjusted for price differences across countries and across time.

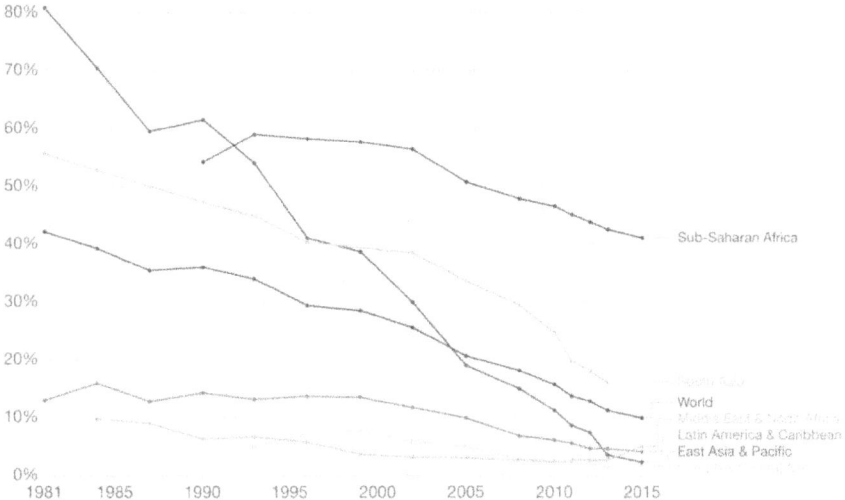

Image 56

After two thousand years with little change in life expectancy, embracing evidence-based lifestyles and healthcare finally improved lifespans in a way that religious leadership and prayer rituals had never been able to – yet another reason why humanity is turning away from religion and towards science to improve their lives.

Life expectancy, 1770 to 2015

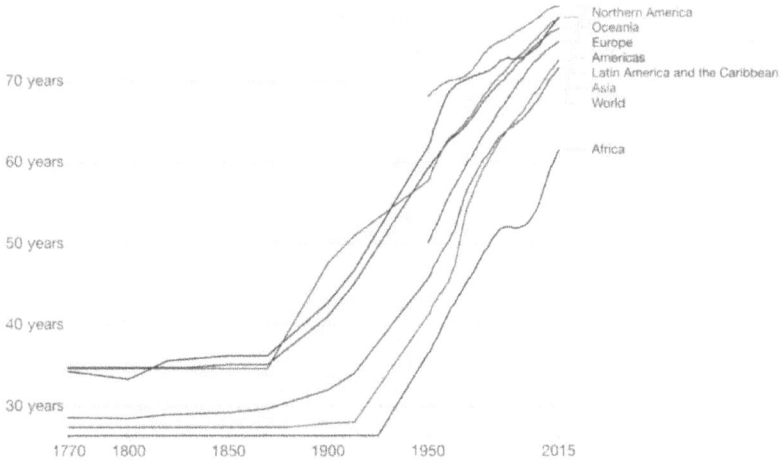

Northern America
Oceania
Europe
Americas
Latin America and the Caribbean
Asia
World

Africa

70 years

60 years

50 years

40 years

30 years

1770   1800   1850   1900   1950   2015

Source: Riley (2005), Clio Infra (2015), and UN Population Division (2019)   OurWorldInData.org/life-expectancy · CC BY
Note: Shown is period life expectancy at birth, the average number of years a newborn would live if the pattern of mortality in the given year were to stay the same throughout its life.

Image 57

Schooling

Aristotle famously said, "Give me a child until he is seven and I will show you the man," thereby highlighting the key role of education in shaping lives and communities. For a society to become less tribalistic but increasingly open-minded and welcoming, changes are required to current education systems.

Within their own homes, people are by all means entitled to inculcate their own belief systems and cultural ties in their children. But tax-payer-funded schools should not be allowed to enforce any particular religious outlook. It is important to educate our children about religions, but the teaching needs to have a historical and cultural perspective rather than seeking to convert students to one or another religion. If children were taught about all religions, they would quickly realize that each one is not "special" or "correct", but merely a cultural practice. The idea that any one religion is right while others are false would be seen for the absurdity that it is.

Even the use of school premises by religious groups outside regular hours should not be permitted; religions have enough properties of their own where they can preach their doctrines.

In some parts of the world, there appears to be confusion as to the social purpose of school systems. Often there is uproar when politicians discuss legislating against religious education in schools. It is apparent that parents who protest vehemently against removing religion from curricula ignore the fact that schools are now multicultural. Children should not be indoctrinated into only their parent's narrow worldview. That can happen outside school hours. The aim of schooling should be to produce more inquiring and questioning minds rather than narrow-minded perspectives.

The challenges of integrating immigrants into a new society are exacerbated by families who want their children to attend a narrow education system based on their own culture or religion. If all children were allowed to mix freely with children from other backgrounds, integration would be a faster, smoother process and new arrivals would be more readily accepted by their adopted communites.

Nor should schools allow local religious leaders to have a say in school curricula, particularly when it comes to the way sex education is taught. These are universal concerns and we do our children a great disservice by allowing clergy to meddle in this arena. Religions have long caused great harm by urging their followers to suppress their sexuality and believe that masturbation, pre-marital sex and homosexuality are sinful, resulting in untold guilt and trauma. And of course clerics have perpetrated horrendous sexual offences against countless young people themselves, ironically often as a result of them having to practice the unnatural act of abstinence. It is time for religions to no longer speak to children on this topic.

One way to ensure that religious leaders are no longer seen as arbiters of moral codes would be to introduce regular courses in human ethics. I am constantly disappointed by the lack of ethics programs in schools, and am confident that we would see improved outcomes if they were a part of the curriculum until at least mid-high school. Imagine the creative and considerate human beings such a system could shape compared to the divisive mindsets created by religious precepts. A secular education will undoubtedly result in a more unified, accepting and contented society, as evidenced by such countries as Sweden, where only a very small percentage of schools are religious.

Ironically, a secular society offers the greatest freedom for people to follow and practise whatever faith they want to adopt, even if it is at odds with the dominant creed of that society. Christians living in a predominantly Christian country have little awareness of this and it would be a great reality check for these people to try living as a member of a Christian minority in a non-Christian country. Maybe then they would prefer that the dominant religion not be taught in government schools.

Family law

Where religions are able to "interfere" in personal relationship break-ups, they nearly always favour the male partner, for example when it comes to allowing divorce, or in the divorce settlement itself. This power must be removed from religious organizations so that only the government of a nation can grant and make such determinations.

Clergy were once the proprietors of the social respectability that a religious marriage bestowed, but they are now utilized far less frequently. In the United Kingdom in 1900, religious ceremonies accounted for 85% of all marriages. In the early 1990s that rate fell below 50% and it has been on a consistent decline since then, with now only 23% of marriages being religious. Civil ceremonies now account for three in four marriages across the United Kingdom. The pre-marital role of being a marriage advisor has also all but disappeared.

Percentage of civil and religious ceremonies, England and Wales, 1967 to 2017

Image 58

Something similar is also starting to occur with funeral services. Up until recent times, nearly all ceremonies were hosted by religious leaders, but there are now many humanist and non-denominational funeral parlours providing these services. The proportion of communal functions administered by religious organizations is ever-receding.

The recent marriage equality debates and legal amendments that have occurred in many countries further reflect the general abandonment of religious strictures. The last two decades have seen such a rapid acceptance of non-heterosexuals that many people never expected to see in their lifetimes. So many countries or states within countries have legalized the union of non-heterosexuals within a very short timeframe.

In Poland, where the Catholic Church still wields much power and influence, zones have been created where LGBTQI ideologies are not tolerated. In response to this, US Senator Joe Biden, while running for President of the United States in September 2020 tweeted: "Let me be clear: LGBTQI+ rights are human rights – and 'LGBT-free zones' have no place in the European Union or anywhere in the world."[20] The efforts of religions to suppress human rights in order to enforce their own doctrines are no longer being tolerated in an ever-increasing number of countries, particularly among the young, which is accelerating the repudiation and decline of old ideologies.

Conclusions

There are still too many instances where the predominant religious views influence choices and options within society. It is time for a complete separation of religion and state. Only then will we be able to cooperatively build unified, progressive societies and rationally tackle the many complex issues that lie ahead, including artificial intelligence, euthanasia and stem-cell research.

CHAPTER 7
Closing Thoughts

If the current trends continue, then within 50 years most religions will be mere cultural remnants of the powerful institutions they once were. Associated practices, festivals, buildings and monuments will endure and be utilized, perhaps for another century or so, but the centrality of the concept of a deity and the related archaic teachings will have faded.

By the time Millennials and their descendants comprise most of the human population, dogmatic religious adherents will be fringe-dwellers of society, living in ever-isolated communities, for not only are today's young people turning forcefully against religion they are also becoming increasingly apatheistic.

Nietzsche's phrase that "God is dead" will become an interesting but irrelevant historical perspective, a mere narrative of where humankind was at until the 21st century. As on many other fronts in this millennium, changes will occur more rapidly than expected and the maxim "I didn't expect to see that happen in my lifetime" will assuredly apply to the decline of religions too. There will undoubtedly be some speedhumps along the way and a backwards step here and there, but such things are to be expected on the road of progress.

After thousands of years of being under the influence of religious viewpoints, those societies that most actively institute the secular emancipation of women will become the most successful. Most countries only gave women the ability to vote in the last one hundred years, and inclusion and acceptance of women in the workforce and political systems has been slow. Yet, while there are still pay inequalities and other issues to overcome for women, the pathway is ever improving. The old patriarchal systems that are the backbone of religions are being overthrown, partly because their indoctrinated inequalities are finally being recognized as such.

To make sure the decline of the power and influence of religions continues, especially in fundamentalist countries and communities, there needs to be increasing acceptance of humanistic views. It is now up to individuals, communities, societies, sociologists and governments to create new and enhanced systems that will support the development of positive, reassuring, unifying secular societies. We should be advocating a complete separation of church from state as one of the essentials to achieve this.

Though I will not be here to witness it, at some point in our future, we will look back on religions as having been an important step in human development, but one that was appropriately consigned to the history books sometime in the early third millennium AD. And this will be acknowledged as one of the major achievements of humankind.

ACKNOWLEDGMENTS

This book is all about extrapolation of data from a variety of studies. I would therefore like to thank all those people and agencies who spend their days surveying populations across the globe. Without such data we would not be able to make informed decisions.

A special thank you to Dr Perry Burstin who donated many hours of his free time to read and reread through the various iterations of the manuscript and provide useful advice, as well as his excellent proofreading skills, which helped improve the final product.

I'm also indebted to a group of deep thinkers known as the "Beyond Unicorns" friendship group, who gathered with me to discuss this and similar topics on a regular basis. Our online video calls during the Covid-19 pandemic were always stimulating. I look forward to spending more time with them all again in person!

And thanks, finally, to my editor, Scott Forbes, who aided me so constructively on my first book and I was happy to have collaborate with me again on this follow-up. He provided exceptional advice and feedback to help bring this book to its final position.

If there are any inaccuracies, please feel free to contact me, so that they may be amended for updated versions of the book, via beyondreligionsthebook@gmail.com

ENDNOTES

Chapter 1
[1]   Christopher Hitchens, *God is Not Great: How Religion Poisons Everything*, Allen & Unwin, Sydney, 2007.

Chapter 2
[2]   Neil DeGrasse Tyson, in Roger Bingham, "The Moon, the Tides and Why Neil DeGrasse Tyson is Colbert's God", The Science Network, 20 January, 2011.

Chapter 3
[3]   See https://www.bsa.natcen.ac.uk/media/39293/1_bsa36_religion.pdf

[4]   Pew Research Center, "In U.S., Decline of Christianity Continues at Rapid Pace", 17 October, 2019.

[5]   Presentation at Pew Research Center Conference, "Survey Research and the Study of Religion in East Asia", 11 October, 2017; www.pewresearch.org/wp-content/uploads/sites/7/2017/11/Religion20171117.pdf

[6]   Pew Research Center, "The Age Gap in Religion Around the World", 13 June 2018.

[7]   Pew Research Center, "The Age Gap in Religion Around the World", 13 June 2018.

[8]   See www.state.gov/reports/2019-report-on-international-religious-freedom/azerbaijan/

9   See   www.pewresearch.org/fact-tank/2017/08/09/muslims-and-islam-key-findings-in-the-u-s-and-around-the-world/

10 See   www.theguardian.com/books/2018/mar/20/richard-dawkins-to-give-away-copies-of-the-god-delusion-in-islamic-countries;   www.the-times.co.uk/article/richard-dawkins-will-give-away-the-god-delusion-to-muslims-bx5zzvzl7

11 WIN-Gallup International, Global Index of Religiosity and Atheism, 2012;   https://sidmennt.is/wp-content/uploads/Gallup-International-um-tr%C3%BA-og-tr%C3%BAaleysi-2012.pdf

12 Matt Arbuckle and David M. Konisky, "The Role of Religion in Environmental Attitudes", *Social Science Quarterly*, November 2015; www.researchgate.net/publication/284113257_The_Role_of_Religion_in_Environmental_Attitudes

13 Twitter feed "@SudanPMHamdok", 12 August 2020.

14 MEMO (Middle East Monitor), 7 September 2020; www.middleeast-monitor.com/20200907-sudan-separates-religion-from-state-ending-30-years-of-islamic-rule/

15 AFP, "Lebanon's President Aoun Calls for Proclamation of 'Secular State'", Al Arabiya, 30 August 2020; https://english.alarabiya.net/en/News/middle-east/2020/08/30/Lebanon-s-President-Aoun-calls-for-procla-mation-of-secular-state

Chapter 4

16 Address at the Conference on Cosmic Design, American Association for the Advancement of Science, Washington DC, April 1999.

Chapter 5

17 https://humanists.international/what-is-humanism/the-amster-dam-declaration/

18 Karl Marx, *Critique of Hegel's Philosophy of Right*, Deutsch–Französische Jahrbücher, 1844.

19 To view the CNN footage, see www.youtube.com/watch?v=YeFzeNA-HEhU&ab_channel=CNN

Chapter 6

20 Twitter feed "@JoeBiden", 21 September 2020.

ILLUSTRATIONS

www.ingramcontent.com/pod-product-compliance
Lightning Source LLC
Chambersburg PA
CBHW062144020426
42334CB00020B/2507